WELCOME

Dear Goal Setters,

It's Freeway and I want to thank you for considering joining me on this journey of goal setting. Investing in yourself and accomplishing your goals is a tremendous win. It will be an amazing experience to share goal-setting tips and advice with you. Your commitment to self-improvement and your willingness to put in the work to reach your goals are inspiring.
This workbook is designed to help you set and achieve your own personal goals on a step-by-step base.

You can write about your interests, achievements, and outlook on life. This workbook is packed with exercises, tips, and resources to help you get clear on your goals, create a plan of action and stay on track. Plus, there's plenty of room for you to track your progress along the way. If you're ready to take your life to the next level, I invite you to join me in this workbook. It's going to be an exciting journey!

Sincerely,
Freewayricky &
Mychosia

@freewayricky
@freewayricky
@freewayricky1
@visioncoachmy

www.freewaymillionairesclub.com.
www.freewayrickyross.com
www.visiontracker.app
www.mychosia.com

TABLE OF

CONTENTS

DISCLAIMER

chapter one

INVESTING IN YOURSELF

INVESTING IN YOU

Writing out goals is one of the easiest ways to start investing in yourself. By establishing goals, you take charge of the course of your life or your career is another way of investing in yourself. You get focus from having goals. Your choices and actions ought to move you one step closer to reaching those objectives. Setting goals keeps you moving, boosts your happiness, and has a big impact on your life.

There are many reasons to invest in yourself. Perhaps the most important reason is that when you invest in yourself, you're investing in your future. When you improve your skills, set goals, and seek knowledge, and abilities, you're setting yourself up for success down the road. You will be able to achieve any task that you set your mind to. You will be successful and happy in all that you do.

"Investing in yourself will be one of the most valuable tasks you can ever complete in your lifetime"
-Sharon D. Oats

Another reason to invest in yourself is that it makes you happier. When you're happier, you're more productive, and you have more energy. People who are invested in themselves are also more satisfied with their lives.

Finally, investing in yourself is a good way to stay ahead of the competition. As the world changes, it becomes increasingly important to keep up with the latest trends and technologies. By investing in yourself, you'll be better equipped to compete in today's economy.

BENEFITS TO INVESTING IN YOURSELF

Standard benefits:

-Improved Mental Health: Investing in yourself helps to increase your self-confidence and self-esteem. It can also help you to gain clarity and focus, allowing you to better manage stress and prioritize your goals.

-Increased Professional Skills: Investing in yourself through education and training can help you to gain new skills and increase your overall knowledge base, which can help you to advance in your career.

-Increased Happiness: Investing in yourself can help to increase your overall happiness as you become more confident and secure in yourself. This can lead to increased satisfaction in your personal and professional life.

-Improved Productivity: Investing in yourself can help you to become more productive as you learn new strategies and approaches to tackle challenges and complete tasks more efficiently.

-Increased self-awareness: Investing in yourself can help you gain a better understanding of your strengths, weaknesses, and interests. This knowledge can help you make better decisions about your career and life goals.

- Having specific goals to work towards will help you stay focused and motivated.

- Writing down your goals makes them more concrete and achievable.
- Achieving your goals will give you a sense of accomplishment and pride.

-Richer relationships: Investing in yourself can help you build better relationships with others. It can help you be a better listener, communicator, and friend.

Emotional benefits:

- Setting goals allows you to dream big and aim high.
- Reaching your goals will give you a feeling of control over your life and destiny.

-Improved self-esteem: Investing in yourself can help you feel proud of your accomplishments and more confident in yourself. It can also help you overcome feelings of inadequacy or low self-worth.

There are many reasons to invest in yourself. Perhaps the most important reason is that when you invest in yourself, you're investing in your future. When you improve your skills, set goals, and seek knowledge, and abilities, you're setting yourself up for success down the road.

Some ways to invest in yourself are by taking classes, reading books, and practicing meditation or mindfulness.

All of these can help you learn new things and develop new skills

Additionally, investing in yourself can boost your self-confidence and happiness, which in turn can improve your overall well-being

So, investing in yourself is definitely a worthwhile endeavor! There are many different ways to do this, so find what works best for you. Maybe you could take some classes to learn new things, or read more books to expand your knowledge. You could also try practicing meditation or mindfulness to improve your mental well-being. whatever you choose, just make sure that it's something that you're really interested in and that you'll stick with.

It's important to set some time aside each month to focus on yourself. This could be a day where you don't work, don't do any chores, and simply relax and enjoy your own company. Alternatively, you could use this day to do something that you enjoy or that is beneficial for your mental health, like reading, Taking an online finance class, or listening to a leadership lecture will not only be beneficial to you but only adds to your highly valued self.

As part of my monthly self-care day, I will do the following:

1) Get plenty of restful sleep.
2) Eat healthy foods that make me feel good.
3) Exercise to keep my heart rate strong
4) Spend time with people who make me happy.
5) Take some time for me to relax and recharge.
6) Feed my mind with literature pertaining to my goals

Taking some time for yourself each month is a great way to recharge and de-stress. One great way to recharge and de-stress is by spending time outside in nature. Playing tennis is not just to be competitive.

Whether you go for a walk in the park, sit by a river, or hike in the mountains, getting outside and surrounded by green space can be incredibly calming and rejuvenating.

Another great way to recharge and de-stress is by practicing meditation or mindfulness. Sitting in silence and focusing on your breath can be a great way to center yourself and let go of any stress or anxiety you may be feeling. Some other great ways to recharge and de-stress are by doing yoga or stretching, listening to calming music, or aromatherapy.

Whatever works for you, find what relaxes you and try to make time for it regularly. You may be surprised at how much it can help improve your overall well-being when you set goals for yourself.

By setting goals for yourself, you can work towards becoming the best possible version of yourself. Some goals you may want to consider include: becoming more competitive, increasing your bank account, or becoming more proficient in a certain skill. Whatever your goals may be, make sure to stay motivated and focused on achieving them!

One way to invest in yourself is to create realistic goals. Having specific and measurable goals will help you stay on track and make progress. Some things to consider when creating your goals:

- What do you want to achieve?
- What are your priorities?
- What are your strengths and weaknesses?
- What can you realistically achieve in the given timeframe?
- How will you measure your progress?

WAYS TO INVEST IN YOURSELF

1. Invest in Your Education: Investing in yourself through education can lead to higher salaries, more job opportunities, and better job satisfaction. Consider taking classes, attending conferences and seminars, or getting a degree or certification in your field of interest.

2. Put Money in Your Retirement: Investing in your retirement by saving and investing in the future can help you stay financially secure and prepare you for a comfortable retirement. Consider setting up a retirement account, such as a 401k or IRA, and contributing regularly.

3. Develop Marketable Skills: Investing in yourself by developing your skills can make you more desirable to employers and can open up more job opportunities. Consider taking courses, attending workshops and seminars, or even doing an internship to gain relevant experience. Attend a retreat to focus on personal growth: Consider attending a retreat that focuses on personal growth and self-improvement. This can be a great way to get away from your everyday routine and dedicate time to focus on your growth.

4. Take Care of Your Health: Investing in your health is one of the best investments you can make. Consider eating healthy, exercising regularly, getting enough rest, and seeing your doctor for regular checkups.

5. Invest in Your Network: Investing in your professional network can help you build relationships with influential people, increase your visibility, and create career opportunities. Consider attending networking events, joining professional organizations, and using social media to connect with others.

6. Set Goals: First and foremost, it is important to set goals for yourself in order to know what you want to accomplish. Setting goals will help you stay motivated and focused on your investments.. Set and track goals to stay motivated and focused: Set goals for yourself and track your progress to stay motivated and focused on achieving them. Break down your goals into smaller, achievable tasks and track your progress.

7. Take Time for Yourself: Taking time for yourself is incredibly important when it comes to investing in yourself. Whether it's taking a yoga class, going for a walk, or even just taking some time to relax and reflect, taking time for yourself will allow you to recharge and gain a clearer perspective on what you want to accomplish.

8. Spend Money on Experiences: Investing in yourself doesn't always have to mean spending money on things like education or books. Spending money on experiences such as travel or a cooking class can be just as beneficial.

9. Invest in your relationships: Strengthening and maintaining relationships is key to personal growth. Invest in relationships with friends, family, and mentors to foster meaningful connections.

10. Invest in your career: Investing in your career can mean anything from attending networking events to furthering your education. Take the time to research and understand the opportunities and challenges in your industry.

WAYS TO INVEST IN YOURSELF

11. Take time for yourself to relax and recharge: Take time for yourself to relax and recharge. This can be anything from taking a walk to meditating, to watching a movie. Whatever helps you recharge, make sure to take the time to do it.

12. Develop healthier habits and routines to prioritize self-care: To prioritize self-care, develop healthier habits and routines. This can include anything from getting more sleep to eating healthier, to exercising regularly.

13. Develop a mentor relationship with someone who can help you grow: Find someone who has the knowledge and experience to help guide you on your personal growth journey. Ask them questions, take their advice, and look to them as a source of knowledge and support.

14. Start a journaling practice to reflect on your progress: Journaling can be a great way to reflect on your progress and stay motivated. Spend some time each day or week journaling about your successes, challenges, and areas of improvement.

15. Read books on self-improvement and personal development: Take time to read books that will help you improve yourself, such as books on personal development, self-help, and other topics related to personal growth.

`6. Take a class or workshop to expand your skillset: Invest in yourself by taking classes or workshops in areas that you are interested in, or ones that can help you advance in your career. Look for online classes, or classes at local universities or community colleges.

17. Practicing mindful meditation and positive affirmations can help you to stay focused on your goals, be more present in the moment, and cultivate feelings of gratitude, contentment, and peace. To do this, you can try guided meditations or sitting in silence for a few minutes each day while focusing on your breath. Additionally, writing down a few positive affirmations each day can help to remind you of your strengths and capabilities and promote feelings of confidence and self-love.

18. Learning how to better manage your stress and emotions is a valuable skill that can help you to stay focused on your goals. This could include trying out different stress-reduction techniques, such as deep breathing, progressive muscle relaxation, or yoga. Additionally, it's important to also practice self-awareness and work on identifying and understanding your emotions.

19. Making time to engage in activities that bring you joy can help to keep you motivated and inspired. This could be anything from playing a sport, painting, or baking. It's important to make time every day to do something that makes you happy and brings a sense of fulfillment.

WAYS TO INVEST IN YOURSELF

20. Making a plan to invest in yourself financially can help you to achieve your goals and create a brighter future. This could include things like setting up a budget, creating an emergency fund, paying off debt, or investing in stocks and bonds. Additionally, you could look into ways to earn more money or look for ways to save money.

21. Establishing better boundaries in relationships can help to ensure that you are taking care of yourself and your relationship with others. This means setting limits on how much time and energy you are willing to give to others and being clear about your expectations. It's important to remember that boundaries are not meant to be punitive but instead provide a framework for healthy relationships.

22. Investing in experiences to enrich your life can help you to stay connected to your goals and motivated. This could include travel, attending conferences and workshops, or taking classes. Experiences like these can help to broaden your horizons and provide you with new skills and knowledge.

23. Developing a habit of lifelong learning can help you to stay motivated and on track with your goals. This could include reading books, taking classes, or attending seminars and workshops. Learning is a lifelong process and it's important to continue to educate yourself and stay up to date with new developments in your field.

24. Starting a side-hustle to generate extra income can help to give you financial freedom and open up new opportunities. This could include things like freelancing, starting a blog, or selling products online. It's important to research and determine what type of side-hustle is best for you and create a plan to make it successful.

25. Surround yourself with positive people: Find a support system of positive people who can motivate and encourage you. Avoid negative people who will bring you down.

26. Reward yourself: celebrate your successes along the way. Acknowledge your hard work by rewarding yourself with small treats or special privileges.

27. Develop a routine: Establish a regular schedule of activities that will help you stay focused and productive. Set aside specific times for working on your goals and stick to them.

READING LOG

Title	Author	Date

EMPOWER SELF TALK CAN BE INTERNAL AND EXTERNAL

Start by writing down your personal growth goals. Then, use empowering self-talk to help motivate yourself to achieve these goals. For example, "I can do this" or "I am strong enough to achieve my goals." Repeat these statements to yourself every day, and you will start to see results in your personal growth.

Remember that it's important to be patient and consistent with your self-talk. Don't expect overnight results; allow yourself time to grow and improve. The empowered self-talk will help you stay focused on your goals and make progress toward achieving them.

.External self-talk can also come in the form of encouragement from others. When you have people who believe in you and support your goals, it can be a great motivator to keep moving forward. So don't be afraid to reach out for help and encouragement from those around you. With their support, you can achieve anything!

Internal self-talk is the dialogue that we have with ourselves on a regular basis. This can be either positive or negative, and it can have a huge impact on our personal growth. It's important to be aware of our internal dialogue and to make sure that it is encouraging and motivating. If our internal self-talk is negative, it can hold us back from achieving our goals.
When we receive positive external self-talk, it can boost our confidence and help us to achieve our goals. However, when we receive negative external self-talk, it can have the opposite effect and discourage us from reaching our potential.

Journal Moment

Identify your self-talk and write a positive affirmation statement to replace them.

YOUR NUMBER-ONE ENEMY

1. Procrastination

- Set simple, achievable goals to avoid putting things off
- Create a timeline and stick to it
- Divide tasks into smaller, more manageable parts
- Make sure the task is worth your time and effort
-Create a positive environment that encourages productivity
- Reward yourself for completing tasks
- Often leads to missed deadlines and goals that are never achieved.

2. Perfectionism

Perfectionism can be your worst enemy because it can lead to procrastination and self-doubt. When you're perfectionistic, you may never feel like your work is good enough, which can lead to putting things off until the last minute or never finishing them at all. You may also doubt your ability to do anything well, which can keep you from trying new things or taking risks.

3. People-pleasing

The reason my number one enemy is people-pleasing is that it can take away from my own wants and needs. When I'm always focused on what other people want or need, I'm not focusing on what I want or need, and that can lead to frustration and unhappiness.

4. Unrealistic Expectations

Setting unreasonably high expectations can be discouraging and lead to feelings of failure and powerlessness.

5. Fear of failure/rejection

There are a few reasons why the fear of failure or rejection can be our number one enemy. For one, it can keep us from taking risks and pursuing our dreams, which can ultimately lead to a very unhappy and unfulfilled life. Additionally, fear of failure or rejection can cause us to doubt ourselves and our abilities which can lead to self-esteem issues. Lastly, fear of failure or rejection can cause us to avoid social situations and relationships, which can be isolating and lead to loneliness.

6. Self-judgement.

When it comes to self-improvement, our number one enemy is self-judgment. When we're hard on ourselves, it's often because we're trying to motivate ourselves to do better. But being too critical can actually backfire, making us feel worse and less motivated. Focus on your strengths and give yourself credit for your progress.

7. Low Self-Confidence

Low self-esteem and lack of confidence can lead to a lack of effort and negative self-talk.

8. Poor Time Management

skills can lead to missed deadlines and a lack of progress toward goals.

9. Overwhelm

When faced with too many goals or tasks, it can be difficult to focus and prioritize appropriately.

10. Negative talk

may hold us back from achieving our goals and dreams. It can keep us trapped in a cycle of self-doubt and fear. To break free, we need to start believing in ourselves and our abilities. We need to focus on what we want to achieve, and not let negative thoughts get in the way. What are some things that you have said to yourself that may have held you back from achieving your goals and dreams? Write them down.

"I'm not good enough."
"I can't do it."
"It's too hard."

11. Lack of focus

it is easy to get lost in the distractions of everyday life and lose focus on what is important. This can hold us back from achieving our goals and dreams. However, with a little bit of effort, we can all stay focused on what is important to us.

Here are a few tips to help you stay focused:

a) Set aside time each day to work on your goal or dream. Dedicate this time specifically to working on your goal, and don't let yourself get interrupted.

b) Remove distractions from your environment. Turn off your phone, close your laptop, and put away any other distractions that might keep you from focusing.

c) Make a plan. Having a plan helps you stay focused and prevents you from getting overwhelmed. Break down your goal into smaller steps and make a timeline for completing each step.

d) Stay positive. It can be tough to stay focused when things aren't going the way you want them to, but it's important to stay positive and keep pushing forward. Remember why you set your goal in the first place, and think about how good it will feel when you finally achieve it."

12. Unclear Goals

If your goals are vague or undefined, it is difficult to know how to proceed and measure success.

13. Lack of Resources

Having access to the right tools, skills, and support can be essential to achieving goals.

14. Unsupportive Environment

Having an unsupportive or hostile environment can make it difficult to stay focused and motivated.

15. Distractions

It can be easy to get distracted by other activities or responsibilities, leading to a lack of focus on the goal.

16. Poor Planning

Without a clear plan of action, it's difficult to measure progress and stay on track.

Personal Goals Examples That can help you

PERSONAL GOALS

1. Develop a healthier lifestyle.
2. Exercise regularly.
3. Practice mindfulness.
4. Take time to relax and reduce stress.
5. Set and achieve personal goals.
6. Build strong relationships with friends and family.
7. Learn a new skill or hobby.
8. Reduce and manage debt.
9. Take care of your physical health.
10. Develop a daily routine.
11. Improve your communication skills.
12. Develop a positive attitude.
13. Find balance in your life.
14. Prioritize your tasks and manage your time.
15. Develop a healthy self-image.
16. Learn to trust and forgive yourself.
17. Pursue personal growth.
18. Develop financial planning skills.
19. Develop your creativity.
20. Develop a personal mission statement.
21. Set and achieve academic goals.
22. Pursue higher education.
23. Take risks and challenge yourself.
24. Become more organized.
25. Take care of your mental health.
26. Develop a good work-life balance.
27. Learn to say "no" to things you don't want.
28. Learn new technology.
29. Find your passion.
30. Network with others.
31. Create a budget.
32. Take care of your spiritual health.
33. Read more books.
34. Develop a growth mindset.

35. Become more independent.
36. Volunteer in your community.
37. Improve your problem-solving skills.
38. Set boundaries and stick to them.
39. Join a support group.
40. Take initiative and be proactive
41. Develop a good study routine.
42. Take responsibility for your own decisions.
43. Make time for self-care and relaxation.
44. Build a support system.
45. Make time for fun.
46. Learn to be assertive.
47. Set goals and create an action plan to achieve them.
48. Develop positive coping skills.
49. Develop a good sleep routine.
50. Practice self-discipline.
51. Spend time in nature.
52. Participate in a hobby or activity you enjoy.
53. Improve your listening skills.
54. Develop a good money management plan.

PERSONAL GOALS

55. Become more resourceful.
56. Develop better self-awareness.
57. Develop better self-confidence.
58. Take ownership of your mistakes.
59. Practice gratitude.
60. Eat healthier foods.
61. Reduce clutter.
62. Take up a new language.
63. Learn to say "no" to others.
64. Develop better self-control.
65. Reduce unnecessary expenses.
66. Stand up for yourself.
67. Develop better decision-making skills.
68. Get more involved in your community.
69. Learn to be flexible.
70. Learn to manage your emotions.
71. Develop a sense of purpose.
72. Improve your public speaking skills.
73. Develop a better work ethic.
74. Be more open to change.
75. Take on new challenges.
76. Become more creative.
77.Developbetter time management skills.
78. Look for new opportunities.
79. Set healthy boundaries.
80. Learn to trust others.
81. Pursue a healthier lifestyle.
82. Spend time with people who bring out the best in you.
83. Learn to forgive.
84. Develop better problem-solving skills.
85. Create an emergency fund.
86. Get involved in a cause you believe in.
87. Invest in yourself.
88. Practice self-love.
89. Take a course or class.
90. Improve your writing skills.
91. Invest in your education.

92. Develop better self-esteem.
93. Appreciate what you have.
94. Make time for yourself.
95. Find a mentor.
96. Start a side hustle.
97. Develop a good work-life balance.
98. Learn to be optimistic.
99. Become more confident.
100. Learn to accept criticism
101. Develop a good social media etiquette.
102. Learn to accept compliments.
103. Find ways to stay motivated.
104. Learn to be patient.
105. Develop better communication skills.
106. Make time for hobbies and activities you enjoy.
107. Develop a good budgeting plan.
108. Improve your listening skills.
109. Practice self-compassion.
110. Be open to new experiences.
111. Develop good habits.
112. Learn to say "no" to people.
113. Take a break from technology.
114. Learn to trust yourself.
115. Develop better emotional intelligence.

PERSONAL GOALS

116. Find a healthy way to express yourself.
117. Find a support system.
118. Make time to connect with nature.
119. Get rid of toxic relationships.
120. Spend time with people who make you happy.
121. Take steps to achieve your goals.
122. Develop a better understanding of yourself.
123. Learn to be more assertive.
124. Develop an attitude of gratitude.
125. Take responsibility for your actions.
126. Practice positive self-talk.
127. Find a passion project.
128. Find a way to give back.
129. Take ownership of your life.
130. Improve your networking skills.
131. Challenge yourself to try something new.
132. Set and achieve professional goals.
133. Develop a good work ethic.
134. Learn to manage stress.
135. Learn to be more open-minded.
136. Develop better self-discipline.
137. Set aside time for reflection.
138. Learn to prioritize your tasks.

139. Take control of your finances.
140. Practice self-care.
141. Pursue a meaningful career.
142. Develop a better understanding of others.
143. Learn to be more flexible.
144. Take a risk and challenge yourself.
145. Develop a positive outlook.
146. Develop good organizational skills.
147. Develop better listening skills.
148. Pursue your dreams.
149. Learn to be more independent.
150. Find ways to stay motivated and inspired.

chapter two

WHAT IS GOAL SETTING

WHAT IS GOAL SETTING

Setting goals is a key component of success. A goal acts as a compass, pointing us in the direction of who we are and where we want to go. It permits us to concentrate our efforts in order to accomplish the goals that are most important. Nothing on earth can prevent you from attaining your goal if you are clear about it. Success without objectives is like traveling aimlessly.

A goal is a specific destination. We intend to accomplish that in the future. Setting objectives is the first step in deciding to work toward them. But you have to start if you want to make and meet goals. It's clearly up to you what you want to accomplish for yourself or your family.

It's hard to set goals, but it is critical for success - how could we accomplish anything without a target? So many people fail because they set goals and don't take action or take inadequate action. But I'm going to help you learn how to set and reach your goals.

DEFINE YOUR GOAL FOR THE TYPE OF LIFE YOU WANT

Goal setting is the process of identifying a specific, desired outcome and establishing the necessary steps to achieve it. It is a form of self-investment that can help you stay motivated and focused on achieving your goals. Goal setting involves setting short-term and long-term goals, making a plan for achieving them, and taking action to make your goals a reality. Through goal setting, you can learn to prioritize your time and resources, stay organized, and establish a plan for success.

You use the goal-setting process to identify your objectives and develop a strategy for accomplishing them. Setting goals is only one aspect of goal setting.
It involves planning a methodical strategy for accomplishing your objectives, one that incorporates tiny, gradual stages as well as benchmarks and successes to keep you inspired along the way. Grab a tab or a pen, and let's tackle this together.

THE TRUTH ABOUT GOAL SETTING

Goal setting can be a powerful tool for achieving success. It helps you to focus your energy and resources on what you want to achieve and gives you a sense of purpose and direction. Goal setting can also help you develop a greater sense of self-awareness, recognize your strengths and weaknesses, and create a plan for success. When you set goals, you can also develop a greater sense of personal accountability, build discipline, and increase your motivation. Setting goals can also help you stay organized and prioritize tasks, as well as develop better problem-solving and decision-making skills. Finally, goal setting can help you manage stress and anxiety, as you have a clear plan to follow.

The truth about goal setting is that it's not enough to simply set a goal and hope for the best. In order to achieve your goals, you need to take specific actions and put in the work. If you're not willing to do that, then your goals are probably not worth achieving.

One of the most crucial choices you can make in life is setting goals. Most people
take an effort to make clear, personal goals for their lives. You need to think about where you want to be in a month, a year, or ten years. The greatest method to make sure you're on the right track and prevent pursuing goals that don't excite you is to take the time to choose where you want to go.

People who don't set goals for their lives may feel they have little control over them, which makes them extremely dependent on the people and situations in their environment as they drift through life. Instead of leveraging the environment to create the experiences, they give authority to it.

As a result, individuals don't accomplish as much as they could if they had organized their life and set clear goals. Nevertheless, it's crucial to keep in mind that having goals alone is insufficient. It can be just as harmful to have unclear goals that are inconsistent with your personal values as it is to have no goals at all

It's unfortunate that many people who take the effort to make objectives spend years working toward one thing only to realize afterward that it wasn't what they really wanted. Your intrinsic drive, live autonomy, mastery, or purpose can all be accessed by setting the right goals.

This workbook will help you identify your objectives and the kind of life you wish to lead by self-discovering the work you need to do. Take your time to fill in all of the blank spaces needed to achieve your goal from the action list, mind mapping, journaling, and tracking your own progress.

Goal setting is a framework for success. How can you be successful if you don't know what you want? A goal is like a compass that guides us toward who we are and where we are going. It enables us to focus our time and resources so that we can achieve the things that matter most. If you know your goal, there is nothing on this earth that can stop you from achieving it. Success without goals is a journey without direction.

Goals are essential for any successful journey. Goals provide motivation and direction and help you to focus on the steps necessary to achieve your desired outcome. Setting goals will help you to create a plan of action and stay on track to reach your desired destination. Without goals, you may find yourself aimlessly wandering, or worse, stuck in a rut. Goals provide a sense of purpose and direction and ensure that you are working towards something, rather than simply drifting through life. Without goals, you may find yourself feeling lost or unsure of what to do next. Setting goals and taking action will give you a greater sense of control over your life and help you to move forward with confidence.

SHORT TERM GOAL

What resources do you need to reach these goals?

Develop a plan for how to invest in yourself for personal growth:

SHORT TERM GOAL

What timeline do you need to set for yourself to reach each goal?

What specific areas of personal growth do you want to focus on?

What steps will you take to achieve these goals?

Set goals. Work hard.
Hustle.

Celebrate your wins.

Repeat the cycle.

VISION BOARD

VISION BOARD

Investing in yourself is one of the most important things you can do in life. It can help you reach your goals, become more successful, and ultimately, live a better life. One way to invest in yourself is to create a vision board. A vision board is a visual representation of your goals, dreams, and aspirations. It is a way to keep yourself motivated and on track to achieving those goals. It is like a roadmap for your life and helps you stay motivated and on track to achieve your goals. With a vision board, you can easily visualize what you want to accomplish and make sure you are taking the necessary steps to reach those goals.
There are benefits to using a vision board for investing in yourself.

The benefits of a vision board include 1. Clarity: creating a vision board provides clarity and focus on what you want to achieve. It helps to eliminate distractions and focus on what is truly important to you. 2. Motivation: having a visual representation of your goals can provide motivation and help to keep you on track. Seeing your goals and dreams on a board can be a great reminder and source of inspiration.3. Accountability: having a vision board can provide accountability and help to keep you accountable for your actions.

When you have a physical representation of your goals, it can be a reminder of what you need to do to achieve them. 4. Creativity: a vision board can help to spark creativity and give you ideas for making your goals a reality. You can use it to brainstorm ideas and come up with creative ways to make your goals happen.

Life Wheel

TODAY'S DATE:_______________________________

Life Wheel

HOW TO USE THE LIFE WHEEL

The Level 10 Life, or Life Wheel, is a simple, but powerful tool for self assessment and self reflection. It can also aid in goal setting and allow you to track your progress in the major areas of your life. In essence, it's a visual representation of how balanced your life is.

SETTING UP YOUR WHEEL

Label each section with a life area. This is totally particular to your life and whatever facets are most important to you or take up a good amount of your time and focus. Do what feels best for you. These sections/categories may change as your life unfolds and that is totally fine! Change is inevitable so feel free to change these areas as often as needed to reflect your life now.

Here's some category ideas to get you started:

- Relationships
- Physical
- Health
- Spirituality
- Career/Business
- Finances
- Home Life & Family
- Education
- Mental Health
- Creativity
- Personal Development
- Learning
- Self Development
- Self Care
- Emotional Well-being
- Overall Life Vision
- Marriage/Romantic Relationship
- Parenting

DRAW YOUR WHEEL

You can assign a different color for each category if you choose. After you've labeled each area, think about how fulfilled you are in each life area. Draw a dot between the center of the circle and the outer edge of the wheel to indicate how fulfilled you feel in each life area. The center of the wheel represents 0% and the outer edge represents 100%, or Level 10. After you place all of your dots, color in the areas in between the middle and the outside of the circle, or draw lines from one dot to the next to connect them all together.

REFLECT AND SET MEANINGFUL GOALS

Reflect on the shape of your completed wheel. How can you create a more evenly shaped wheel? Which life areas need more of your focus right now? You can start with the lowest points of your wheel or focus on the high points first and work your way to the lower points - whichever way feels best to you. After some reflection, set goals for each area of your life. There's always room for growth so make sure to set goals for every life area even if you rated yourself highly in that category.

You can complete your life wheel as often as you'd like to track your progress and measure your overall feeling of balance in your life. It's also a good tool to use when something just feels 'off' in your life, but you're not exactly sure why you're feeling that way.

ASSESSMENT

WHAT AREAS WOULD U LIFE TO IMPROVE ON

Relationships	
Health	
Spirituality	
Career/Business	
Finances	
Home Life & Family	
Education	
Personal Development	
Emotional Well-being	
Overall Life Vision	
Romantic Relationship	
Self Care	

chapter three

THE IMPORTANCE OF GOAL SETTING

THE IMPORTANCE OF GOAL SETTING

Setting goals is one of the most important things you can do for yourself. When you have a goal, you have something to aim for, and this can help you to stay focused and motivated.

There are a few things to keep in mind when setting goals:

1. Make sure your goals are realistic and achievable. If your goal is too challenging or unrealistic, you may become discouraged and give up.

2. Make sure your goals are specific. Saying "I want to be healthier" is not as specific as saying "I want to eat more fruits and vegetables every day."

3. Make sure your goals are time-bound. Giving yourself a timeline for reaching a goal will help you stay on track.

4. Make sure your goals are meaningful to you. If you don't really care about reaching a goal, it will be harder to stay motivated.

When setting goals, it's important to be patient and not expect too much too soon. Rome wasn't built in a day, and you won't reach your goals overnight either! But if you stick with it and make goal-setting a regular part of your life, you will see results over time.

When it comes to moving forward in our lives, we need a purpose. We need the motivation to move forward, this is where setting goals become necessary. And when we have this goal in front of us, it's easier to keep going. I think that everyone should set their own goals and go after them. There are times when the path will be difficult and even seem impossible to step forward. But if someone believes in what they're doing, they'll find a way to reach their goal.

In life, you have dreams. Often times they are out of reach and you question if they will ever come true. Not all goals have a definite time frame or a tangible result. Goals must be focused on with clarity, enthusiasm, and action.

It's great how much you can accomplish when you have goals. When we have goals, it acts as a guiding force and helps us make decisions. By setting goals you can direct the outcome of your life. Setting goals is a very important part of our lives. It helps us achieve the things we want to achieve in life. We do many things for this reason. I will tell you what is the importance of setting goals. And how you can have a great goal-setting. Setting goals is hard work, but the results can be amazing.

Setting goals directs your subconscious mind, assisting you in achieving your objectives. They provide you with a life path. Setting vague goals such as "I want to make more money" or "I want to live a happy life" will not lead to a fulfilling life. Your subconscious is a powerful machine, and understanding how it works is an important part of setting successful goals.

You know that you need to set goals in order to achieve success, but sometimes it's hard to know where to start. The best way to start goal setting is by breaking it down into small, manageable steps. Our free goal-setting worksheet will help you do just that. With this easy-to-use guide, you'll be able to create attainable goals and track your progress along the way. Start achieving your dreams today!

By focusing on outcomes, "you" provide the objective. Your automatic mechanism then provides the means. Your subconscious mind acts similarly to a GPS system in that it continuously searches the surroundings for data related to the information you've provided. Because of this, you will have a better chance of success if you set clear targets. Your subconscious mind receives a powerful signal that enables it to use its focus to find possibilities to accomplish the goal. Some of the significance of setting goals

01
EMPOWERS YOU

When you start setting your own goals in all areas of your life, you stop giving up power rather than allowing others to do so for you. Setting goals for your relationships, finances, career, health and personal life will enable you to regain control and become more empowered. You make the conscious decision to become the creator of your own life and begin to accept responsibility for every aspect of your life. Taking the time to figure out your future goals will significantly impact your life. What if you knew exactly how much money you wanted to make in five years, where you wanted to be in twenty-five years, and how long you wanted to live?

02
IMPROVES SELF-ESTEEM

When you set specific goals for yourself, you can improve your self-esteem. Having clear goals and knowing what you need to do to achieve those goals boosts and reinforces your self-esteem. Part of our self-esteem stems from a desire to see ourselves capable of dealing with life's challenges. This means that with each goal you achieve, you will feel better prepared to deal with other goals and problems in life. High self-esteem is one of the best predictors of personal happiness. One of the most effective ways to boost your self-esteem is consistently achieving your goals.

03
CREATE HEALTHY LIFESTYLE

Setting goals that excite you and are good for your overall health is one of life's best medicines. People who consistently set goals and are unwavering in their pursuit of those goals understand that each time they set a new goal, they are creating a better life. They make a compelling unknown cause that will lead to a more fulfilled and happy life. Setting goals and taking the necessary steps to achieve those goals allows you to shape the future you desire.

CHANGE YOUR LIFE FOR THE BETTER

Setting goals is a worthwhile exercise, whether or not you end up accomplishing them. Setting objectives gives you the chance to consider your future, consider your beliefs, and determine what is most important to you. You'll get clarity and be able to view the larger picture if you set goals. Setting specific goals can help you reconstruct your reality and understand that the dreams you once believed were out of reach are actually within your reach.

Regardless of how ambitious they may be, this process begins when you decide what your true goals are. The process of eliminating your limiting ideas based on prior experiences is started by this activity. It is harder to get the life you want and deserve because of your past restricting beliefs. Setting clear objectives will help.

Be flexible If something isn't working, don't be afraid to adjust your plan. Sometimes the best way to reach a goal is to take a different approach. Don't give up no matter how hard it gets, don't give up. Stay focused on your goal and remember why you're working so hard. Ask for help if you need help, don't be afraid to ask for it. Talking to a friend, family member, or mentor can give you the support and guidance you need to reach your goals.

notes

GET RID OF TOXIC PEOPLE IN YOUR LIFE

Toxic people can have a negative impact on your life and mental health. They can be draining and discouraging, and they can sap your energy and enthusiasm. They can cause stress, worry, and anxiety, and they can also damage your self-esteem and confidence. Removing toxic people from your life can help you to regain a sense of peace and happiness and will give you the opportunity to focus on the positive relationships you have.

Reasons Why to Remove

There are a few reasons why you need to get rid of toxic people when you are seeking personal growth. First, toxic people are often negative and draining. They will not support your journey or help you grow. Second, they can be a danger to themselves and to you. They may be people of low vibration who will bring down your own vibration and hinder your progress. Finally, it is important to surround yourself with positive people who will support and encourage you on your journey.

If you have the ability to dream or achieve your goals, you have the ability to bring your dreams to life. However, toxic people will persistently insist that you cannot do what you want to because the challenges are too great. You need to avoid these types of people. Having self-doubt is common. Additionally, being a human, you may have some self-doubt. Instead of someone who discourages you, you need someone who can help you overcome your doubts.

People Who Feel Entitled

If someone feels entitled, it means that they think they are better than others and deserve special treatment. This can be a very dangerous person to be around, as they may feel like they can do whatever they want without consequences. It is best to stay away from people who feel entitled, as they may not be able to control their anger or aggression.

People placing limits on themselves

People who place limits on themselves are not worth your time. If someone is constantly placing limits on themselves, then it's likely that they will do the same to you. Stay away from them and find people who are more open-minded and willing to explore new opportunities.

INVESTING IN YOUR PROGRAM "YOURSELF"

It's important to invest in yourself and your program. There are different ways to invest in yourself, such as through education, networking, and other resources. Many ways like setting goals, creating a budget, and tracking your progress.

Education: Education is the foundation for success. Investing in your education is the first step toward success. It is important to invest in classes or courses that will help you gain new skills, increase your knowledge base, and reach your goals.

Networking: Networking is essential to success. It provides you with the resources, contacts, and connections you need to succeed. Investing in your network helps you to create relationships with other professionals in your industry, which can open up opportunities for you to grow and advance in your career.

Resources: Investing in resources such as books, magazines, and online courses can help you stay up-to-date on industry trends and best practices. These resources can also provide you with the tools you need to succeed.

Goals: Setting goals is an important part of investing in yourself and your program. Having clear, achievable goals provides you with a roadmap that you can use to measure your progress and stay motivated.

Budget: Creating a budget is essential for long-term success. A budget will help you track your expenses and ensure that you are investing your money in the right places.

Tracking: Tracking your progress is key to success. This can be done through tracking your spending, monitoring your goals, and measuring your success. This will help you stay on track and make sure you are reaching your goals.

Part of investing in yourself deals with taking control of your finances. Budgeting, saving, and investing having an emergency fund and the dangers of relying on credit cards for everyday purchases.

You have to learn how to understand your credit score, pay off debt, and how set financial goals. Mainly how to protect yourself from predatory lenders and how to spot a scam. The point here should have a better understanding of how to manage your finances and be better equipped to make sound financial decisions. Protecting your finances is a representation of yourself.

Most people don't think about their finances until it's too late. It's important to take control of your finances as soon as possible. With some planning and discipline, you can have a secure financial future. In this chapter, we'll discuss the importance of budgeting, saving, and investing, as well as the dangers of relying on credit cards for everyday purchases. We'll also look at understanding your credit score, paying off debt, and setting financial goals. Finally, we'll discuss how to protect yourself from predatory lenders and how to spot a scam.

Budgeting

Budgeting is the key to taking control of your finances. It's important to track your income and expenses to make sure you're living within your means. Create a monthly budget that includes all of your fixed expenses, such as rent, utilities, and car payments. Then, determine how much you'll need to cover other expenses, like groceries, entertainment, and clothing. Once you have a budget in place, it's important to stick to it. This will help ensure that you're not overspending or going into debt.

Saving and Investing

It's also important to save money for a rainy day. A good rule of thumb is to save at least 10% of your income each month. This money should be kept in a savings account that is easily accessible in case of an emergency. Additionally, you should consider investing some of your money in the long term. This will help ensure that your money is growing and you're building wealth for the future. Two books I will highly recommend are "The Richest Man in Babylon" by George S. Clason and "Rich Girl Code" by Christian Annice.

Using Credit Cards

Credit cards can be a useful tool if used responsibly. However, it's important not to rely on them for everyday purchases. The interest rates on credit cards can be high, and it's easy to get into debt if you're not careful. It's best to use credit cards only for emergency situations and to pay them off as soon as possible.

Understanding Your Credit Score

It's also important to understand your credit score. Your credit score is a snapshot of your creditworthiness. It is a number between 300 and 850 that is used to indicate the likelihood that you will repay your debts. A higher number is generally better, as it indicates a lower risk of default. Your credit score is based on factors such as your payment history, the amounts owed, the length of your credit history, types of credit used, and new credit inquiries. It is important to understand your credit score, as it can affect your ability to take out loans, get a credit card, and even rent an apartment or get a job. It is important to check your credit score regularly and do whatever you can to ensure that it is accurate and up to date. Your credit score is a three-digit number that reflects how likely you are to pay back a loan or credit card debt. Your credit score is based on factors such as your payment history, credit utilization, and length of credit history. It's important to keep an eye on your credit score, as it can affect your ability to get a loan or a credit card.

Paying Off Debt

If you find yourself in debt, it's important to pay it off as soon as possible. Start by listing all of your debts and their interest rates. Then, focus on paying off the debt with the highest interest rate first. Once that debt is paid off, move on to the next one. This will help you save money in the long run, as you'll be paying less interest.

Setting Financial Goals

It's also important to set financial goals. These goals should be realistic and achievable. For example, you might set a goal to save a certain amount of money each month or to pay off the debt within a certain timeframe. Having clear financial goals will help you stay on track and reach your financial goals.

Protecting Yourself from Predators

It's also important to protect yourself from predatory lenders. These lenders often target people with poor credit scores and offer them loans with high-interest rates and fees. If you're offered a loan with a high-interest rate, it's best to look for another option. Additionally, it's important to be aware of scams. Be wary of anyone offering "guaranteed returns" or "risk-free investments". Research the lender: Before taking out a loan, research the lender to make sure they are legitimate and not a predatory lender. Ask around, read reviews, and check with the Better Business Bureau to ensure the lender is reputable. Ask questions: Don't be afraid to ask the lender questions about their business practices, fees, and interest rates. Understand the terms: Make sure you understand all the terms of the loan before signing any paperwork. Be sure to read the fine print and ask questions if something is unclear. Compare rates: Shop around to compare rates and terms from different lenders to make sure you're getting the best deal.

Don't be rushed: Don't be pressured into taking out a loan before you're ready. Take your time to make sure you're making a smart decision. Be wary of upfront fees: Be wary of lenders who require high upfront fees or deposits before you can take out a loan. Know your rights: Know your rights when it comes to borrowing money. If you feel like you're being taken advantage of or treated unfairly, make sure to report it.

Taking control of your finances is important for a secure financial future. By following the advice outlined in this chapter, you'll be better equipped to make sound financial decisions. Budgeting, saving, investing, and understanding your credit score are all important steps. Additionally, it's important to pay off debt, set financial goals, and protect yourself from predatory lenders and scams. Taking control of your finances is the key to a secure financial future.

chapter four

CLARITY IN GOAL SETTING

CLARITY

CLARITY IN GOAL SETTING

Do you feel as though you are drifting around in life without a plan?
There is nothing more crucial than clarity when it comes to creating goals and choosing the proper course.
It's what will keep you motivated when times are difficult.
Whether we use our thoughts to help or hurt ourselves, they are strong tools.

clarity checklist

- Clarify your wants and needs
- List all the ideas
- Discover your big why
- Learn how to overcome setbacks

Now that you are aware of the need of having specific goals, it is time to determine what your true aspirations are.
Because they don't know what they want, most people don't take the time to develop goals.
This can be an issue because it's likely that you won't achieve much in life if you don't see what you want.
This makes sense given how busy our lives are.
By the end of the day, you can be so worn out that you have no energy left to think about setting objectives for your life.

CLARITY

DISCOVER WHAT YOUR WANTS AND NEEDS

Everyone has desires, and desires can be incredibly motivating, but they can also quickly get out of control and can drive us in ways that can be detrimental to our health and well-being. A sincere desire to help others can change the world. However, the constant desire for more money and material possessions can be destructive and unfulfilling.

Desire can be a very powerful creative force that pushes us to get out of bed in the morning, to eat, sleep, and work to pay for everything you want and to look after your family. Even your ability to read, relax, watch a movie or listen to music is a product of your desire.

Your entire life is a reflection and expression of what you desire. To avoid your desires becoming destructive, it is essential to understand the difference between what we want and what we need for our survival. It is crucial that you know that your needs are entirely different from your wants.

A need is something that is important for us to live in a way that allows us to truly enrich our lives and that may also contribute to others' happiness. It supports our life at a profound level. This includes food, shelter, clothing, security, fulfilling relationships, new experiences, and a variety of other things.

Wants are things that you don't genuinely need. They are things that you can survive without or things that don't make you truly happy. You may think that getting a bigger house, owning an expensive car, or living a life of abundance and endless free time will make you happy.

CLARITY

You don't need material possessions to convince yourself that you are prosperous and successful; you can experience such things instead. This does not imply that you should try to pass for someone else. Instead, it's critical to get to work on raising your self-worth and overcoming low self-esteem. Your surroundings will start to reflect this internal transformation, and you'll start to see changes outside of your control that can help you expand your material wealth and improve your financial situation.

When you choose a significant life goal, it's crucial to be absolutely honest with yourself about the true, underlying reason why you want to accomplish that objective. Your "Big Why" will serve as a powerful motivating force to guide your life in the direction you desire.

WANTS	NEEDS

DISCOVER YOUR BIG WHY

When you desire something, ask yourself if you actually need it or are just wanting it. Try to ascertain whether you're only resisting an internal transformation or having low self-esteem. The following queries are important to ask.

- Do you really need it to accomplish something worthwhile?
- Is it something that can help other people be happy?

This is a fantastic approach to examining your desires, especially if you have lofty aspirations for the future. When establishing your goals, keep in mind to ask yourself these questions. You may assess whether you actually need something to accomplish your overall life goals or if it's just something you want by using the exercise below.

Write out each of your goals on a piece of paper and add the words "so that" after each one. Following that, you should fill in the reason after the words "so that" to better understand what you want. Continue adding "so that's" until you find your single motivating reason for your goal.

When you go through each of your goals in this manner, you will feel a greater sense of purpose, energy, connection, and passion. These are the feelings you want because they will help you achieve your objectives. Goals become truly unstoppable when fueled by a burning desire or a powerful motivating force.

WHAT IS AN ACCOUNTABILITY PARTNER AND WHY DO YOU NEED ONE

As anyone who's ever tried to stick to a New Year's resolution knows, it can be tough to stay on track without some accountability. That's where an accountability partner comes in. An accountability partner is someone you check in with regularly to help you stay on track with your goals. They can provide support and encouragement, and they can help you stay accountable by holding you accountable for your actions. In short, an accountability partner can be a useful tool for helping you reach your goals. So if you're looking to make a change in your life, consider finding an accountability partner to help you along the way.

An accountability partner can be a valuable asset when it comes to achieving your goals. A good accountability partner will help you stay on track, providing encouragement and support when you need it most. But how do you go about finding the right person for the job? Here are a few things to consider:

First, think about what kind of relationship you're looking for. Do you want someone who is similar to you in terms of personality and interests, or someone who is different? There is no right or wrong answer, but knowing what you're looking for will help you narrow down your options.

Second, consider your mutual goals. What are you both hoping to achieve? Make sure that your goals are compatible before moving forward.

Finally, take some time to get to know each other. Spend time talking, texting, or video chatting so that you can get a sense of whether or not you click. Once you've found someone who meets all of your criteria, ask them if they're interested in being your accountability partner. If they say yes, congratulations! You've just taken an important step towards achieving your goals.

THE BENEFITS OF AN ACCOUNTABILITY PARTNER

We all know how difficult it can be to stay on track with our goals. Whether we're trying to eat healthier, get money, or stay in shape, it's all too easy to let our good intentions fall by the wayside. That's where having an accountability partner comes in. By teaming up with someone who shares your goals, you can help each other stay on track and reach your objectives.

An accountability partner can provide much-needed motivation and encouragement when you're struggling to stay on track. It's also a great way to keep yourself accountable. After all, it's a lot harder to keep the money from unnecessary spending when you know you have to report back to your accountability partner to stay focused. In addition, having someone to share your successes with can make the journey to reaching your goals that much more enjoyable.

So if you're looking for a way to boost your chances of success, consider finding an accountability partner. With a little help from a friend, you'll be well on your way to achieving your goals.

Here are some tips for making the most out of your accountability partner:

1. Be honest with your partner. If you're not honest about your goals, fears, and struggles, your partner won't be able to help you as effectively.

2. Set realistic goals. If you set unrealistic goals, you're setting yourself up for disappointment. Work with your partner to set goals that are achievable and that will help you make progress.

3. Be open to feedback. Feedback from your accountability partner can be invaluable in helping you stay on track. Welcome constructive criticism and use it to improve your performance.

4. Hold each other accountable. Accountability works both ways – make sure you're holding up your end of the bargain by being accountable to your partner as well.

5. Communicate regularly. Check in with your partner frequently to let them know how you're doing and to ask for help when needed. Regular communication will help keep both of you on track.

BIG WHY TRANSFORMATION

Transform your pain points into powerful goals that will motivate you to make the desired change in your life.

WHAT IS YOUR GOAL	WHY YOU WANT TO ACHIEVE
☐ ______	☐ ______
☐ ______	☐ ______
☐ ______	☐ ______
☐ ______	☐ ______
☐ ______	☐ ______
☐ ______	☐ ______
☐ ______	☐ ______
☐ ______	☐ ______

Do you have more courage and a burning desire now that you've clarified what you want and why you want to achieve it? Explain your feelings.

______

______

______

Thoroughly completing this exercise can help you avoid wasting time and energy on goals that aren't as important as you first thought. It can also assist you in infusing more passion and energy into goals that you find to be truly worthwhile, putting you on the fast track to success.

GOAL SETTING ASSESSMENTS

WHAT ARE THE FIVE THINGS YOU COULD BE DOING RIGHT NOW IF YOU HAD THE POWER TO DO SO?

DISCOVER IF THERE IS ANYTHING HOLDING YOU BACK FROM ACHIEVING YOUR GOALS.

DO YOU FIND IT WORTHWHILE TO OVERCOME YOUR FEARS TO ACHIEVE YOUR GOALS? EXPLAIN SO THAT YOU CAN FEEL THE NEEDS TO REACH YOUR GOALS

BIG GOAL SETTING PLAN

GOALS

WHY

MOTIVATION

NOTES

CREATE YOUR DREAM LIFE

The first step for crushing your goals and reaching new heights is to decide what you want in life. Unfortunately, many people aren't clear about what they want. Life is hectic, and very few people take the time to plan their lives thoroughly. However, this step is crucial if you're going to live a life of deep meaning and purpose.If you don't know what you want to achieve in life, you need to take the time to look at all the things in your life that are causing you some form of suffering or dissatisfaction that leads to your wants and needs, as discussed at the beginning of this chapter.

If you're disappointed and frustrated with your job or relationship, or if you are dissatisfied with your weight or health, you can change these things when you set your goals and take consistent daily action.

Anything that causes you to suffer can be transformed into an important goal, one that is the complete opposite of what you've been facing. A lack of clarity is responsible for most of the disappointments in life. If you aren't clear about what you want, then the chances of you drifting through life are high. Exploring your dissatisfactions in life can help you to come up with crystal clear goals.

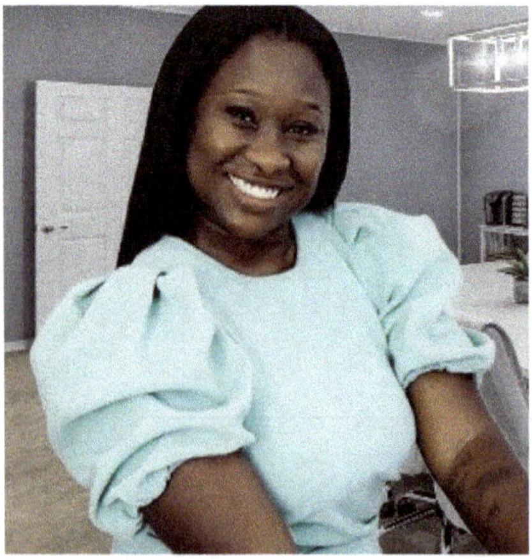

Desire is a fundamental and vital aspect of all life. A strong desire is essential to survive in the world, and it is an essential element in bringing all your goals to fruition.

If you take the time to study the world's most successful people, you see that all their success started with a conscious, crystal clear goal that was fueled by desire. You have to feel emotionally connected to your goals or they will be powerless and difficult for you to achieve. Implementing the below strategies can help you to achieve any of your goals. Become crystal clear on exactly what it is you want and have a strong desire to achieve it.

01 Brainstorming Your Goals

To get a better understanding and clarity of what you want, write out a list of all the things that you would like to achieve during your lifetime. There is no set order that you must follow; the objective is to write down as many goals as possible.

If you find goals later that you don't feel are particularly important, it's okay to cross them off your list. This goes for goals that you're not emotionally connected to as well. You also want to remember to create goals for the major areas of your life, so you don't leave out anything that is important.

02 Creating the Right Mindset

Whether you like it or not, your dominant thoughts, emotions, and beliefs draw into your life positive and negative experiences. This is why it is so important for you to spend your time focusing on positive thoughts as opposed to negative ones.

When you learn to control your inner life, you will be better able to develop the ability to create what you want. The only control you have in your life are the beliefs that you hold, the thoughts that you think, and the actions and reactions you choose.

When you learn how to control your thoughts, feelings, and beliefs, you will have the power to move in any direction that you wish and achieve your biggest dreams. What you believe and think are directly related to how easily and quickly you can achieve your goals.

03

Your Mind Creates your Experiences

Everything that you think, believe, and feel affect your actions, which in turn affect the results you experience during your life. You can waste a lot of your energy and time trying to change your external circumstances, but if you don't change your inner life, then your results may be significantly less than you expected. Changing what you believe to be true, how you think, and how you feel will give you the power to truly steer your life in any direction that you desire and it will provide you with the ability to achieve the life you deserve.

Writing our goals down helps you understand real change which requires real sacrifices. Goals written down are an important step in understanding how to make a change and what sacrifices may be necessary in order to do so. It can help us to be more mindful of our actions and how they lead us closer or further away from our goals. Putting pen to paper, or typing out our goals can also bring clarity and focus to the desired outcome. Writing down goals allows us the opportunity to set parameters for what we want to achieve, and then work towards those objectives.

By taking the time to write down our goals, we are also able to review them regularly, making any necessary modifications or adjustments as time passes. This helps us stay on track with achieving them, as well as allowing us flexibility when needed in order for them to remain realistic, achievable targets. As we review all that has been written, it can also act as a reminder of what's most important; keeping us motivated and focused on our ultimate goal.

Furthermore, writing down goals provides an opportunity for reflection; enabling us to gain insights into why certain outcomes were achieved or why certain obstacles were experienced throughout the process of reaching them. Acknowledging any successes along with any mistakes made gives us valuable insight into how we can continue moving forward efficiently and effectively toward our end goal.

What's more, is that writing down our goals enables us the privilege of committing ourselves completely to achieving the desired result – no matter how challenging or difficult it may seem at first glance – because by doing so we have put into motion a plan that engages both emotional and practical aspects together in unison. This way, when faced with setbacks along the journey, you know exactly what you need to get yourself back on track toward success once again.

AIM YOUR DREAM LIFE

It is important not to rush through this brainstorming session. You may want to have several different brainstorming sessions over time to make sure you include everything. It is essential to come up with a long list of things that you want to achieve throughout your life.

FINANCIAL

FAMILY

HEALTH

RELATIONSHIP

CAREER

PERSONAL GROWTH

Create Spaces Around You

At the point when you permit yourself more space in your everyday routine to simply experience life, you dispense with becoming overwhelmed. You develop an even life for yourself. You make a space to foster one with self and become spiritual. Give yourself the time and the space to intervene, mediate, and eliminate negative energy. Journal an encounter when you made a safe space for yourself.

The day you allow defeat to settle in your mind you have lost the battle before it even started

-Freeway Ricky

OVERCOMING DISAPPOINTMENT AND SETBACKS

For many people, by the time they've reached their late 20s, they've closed down their own ability to dream big because they've had so many disappointments and setbacks in their life. During our childhood, life can seem full of amazing possibilities, and we are excited about what the future holds. However, the harsh realities of life can often knock us down. Relationships that didn't turn out as we had hoped, careers that went wrong, illnesses, and numerous other disappointments are all a part of growing up and learning that life isn't always a bed of roses.

The challenges we face in our lives can enable us to become stronger, wiser, and more capable individuals, or they can cause us to become disillusioned, disempowered, and disappointed in our lives.

The disappointments we encounter in our lives condition us to believe that we will face even more challenges in the future.

Unfortunately, we often experience what we think may happen. Start dreaming big again and start making exciting plans for your future. If you know exactly what it is you want to achieve in your life, congratulations. You're one of the very few individuals who find clarity and know what they truly desire. No matter how motivated you are, there will be times when you face obstacles on your journey to success. Here are some tips for overcoming these setbacks: 1. Acknowledge your challenges: acknowledge your challenges and don't be afraid to ask for help if you need it. 2. Be flexible: be flexible in your approach to achieving your goals. If something isn't working, don't be afraid to try something different. 3. Re-evaluate your goals: take time to re-evaluate your goals and make sure they are still what you want to achieve. 4. Celebrate your progress: celebrate your progress, no matter how small. This will help keep you motivated and inspired.

05
Review Procrastination

Procrastination can be a huge obstacle when trying to achieve your goals. It can keep you from reaching your full potential and prevent you from succeeding. However, there are ways to overcome this common challenge. Here are some tips that should help you get started. We hope that by following these steps, you'll be able to finally put an end to procrastination and achieve the success you deserve.

The first step to ending procrastination when goal setting is to establish a clear goal. This should be something that you are passionate about, and something that you believe will bring you closer to achieving your desired outcome. Once you have identified this goal, break it down into smaller, more achievable tasks. This will help to make the process seem less daunting, and it will also help you stay focused and on track.
Next, create an action plan. This should include specific steps that you need to take in order to reach your goal. Make sure that each task has a due date, as this will make it easier for you to stay motivated and on track. It can also be beneficial to break up larger tasks into smaller sections or milestones so that they can be completed in stages.

Once your plan is in place, start taking action immediately. Don't wait until the day before the deadline – make sure you start right away! Even if it's just taking one small step each day, this progress will add up over time and help keep you motivated and focused on reaching your end goal

.It can also be helpful to set aside some time each day for planning or reflection. This can help keep your motivation levels high by allowing you to review your progress thus far and identify any areas where improvement is needed. Additionally, having regular check-ins with yourself about how close or far away from achieving your goals can provide valuable insights into what strategies are working (or not working).

Finally, don't forget about self-care! Making sure that you take care of yourself physically and mentally is essential when trying to end procrastination and achieve success with goal setting. Self-care activities such as yoga, meditation or journaling can all help reduce stress levels while providing clarity around what needs to be done next in order for the goals at hand to be achieved successfully.

FOCUS ON MY GOAL #1

MAJOR GOALS

IMPORTANT TASKS

OVERCOME SETBACK STRATEGIES

INSPIRATIONAL QUOTES

PROGRESS

FOCUS ON MY GOAL #2

MAJOR GOALS

IMPORTANT TASKS

OVERCOME SETBACK STRATEGIES

INSPIRATIONAL QUOTES

PROGRESS

FOCUS ON MY GOAL #3

MAJOR GOALS

IMPORTANT TASKS

OVERCOME SETBACK STRATEGIES

INSPIRATIONAL QUOTES

PROGRESS

DAILY MINDSET GOALS #1

TOP SPECIFIC GOALS

ACTION STEPS

NOTE TO SELF

PROGRESS

DAILY MINDSET GOALS #2

TOP SPECIFIC GOALS

ACTION STEPS

NOTE TO SELF

PROGRESS

DAILY MINDSET GOALS #3

TOP SPECIFIC GOALS

ACTION STEPS

NOTE TO SELF

PROGRESS

chapter five

ALL ABOUT SMART GOALS

ALL ABOUT SMART GOALS

A goal without a plan is just a wish. You might think you're ready to achieve some pretty big things in life, but it will not happen until you make a concrete plan. What kind of goals are you setting for yourself? Are they in line with your values? Are they worth the time and effort it will take to achieve them? How much time and effort should you be putting into each? If your goals are too small, you may spend your time wishing instead of doing. If they're too big, you might become discouraged or feel that any progress toward your goal isn't enough.

I've been reading about how important it is for people to set goals that are SMART which means specific, measurable, attainable, relevant, and time-bound. Specific and measurable are self-explanatory. Attainable or achievable means that there's a reason for thinking the goal is within reach, it's not just something that sounds nice or seems like it would be fun. Relevant means this goal matters to yo. It's important to your sense of self or how you want to live your life. And time-bound means that you have a deadline in mind for achieving this goal.

Studies show that putting your SMART goals into writing and reviewing them regularly will increase your chances of success. In fact, some studies show that you are as much as 42% more likely to follow through with your goals if you write them down. Writing your goals down will help you get a clear picture of your plan and what you want to accomplish. Logging your goals will also help motivate you to complete the tasks needed in order for success of your goal. Frequently reviewing what you've written will aid in reminding you of your plan, as well as remind you of your "why," in turn, boosting your motivation to keep progressing toward your goal.

WHY YOU NEED TO SET SMART GOALS

We can define goals as objects of a person's ambition or an aim at the desired result. Most of us have some goals set out for ourselves to improve our lives. We can relate your goals to personal or professional progress. Either way, without goals, there's not much room for advancement and without the challenge of reaching a goal you've set for yourself, life would be stagnant. But the process in which we set goals for ourselves matters. Although, you are responsible for whether you follow through with the goals you've set for yourself, how you set them has a hand in determining how successful you'll be in achieving them. The term SMART Goals refers to a process in which you set your goals that will give you greater success.

S The S stands for specific, meaning the goal needs to be clear and specific. When setting a goal for yourself, you must steer away from generalized statements. The more precise the goal is the better.

M Measurable goals refer to tracking your progress. Your goal will be easier met if you can assess progress along the way, giving you more motivation and focus toward your ultimate ambition.

A The A is for attainable. Although your goals should help stretch you outside of your comfort zone and push you to the next level, it's important that the goals you set remain achievable.

R Next R, relevant goals are imperative to your success. This means that the goals you set should be important to you and aligns well with your life and other goals you have set.

T Finally, T, for timely. Your goals should have a deadline to achieve them. This will help keep you on track and focused, and give you opportunities to celebrate your small wins along the way.

Now you already know that SMART is an acronym that stands for Specific, Measurable, Attainable, Relevant and Timely. The SMART goals method will help you with your organization, focus, and clarity with your goals. Research has shown that using the SMART goals method can save you time and simplify reaching your goals. SMART goals are easy to implement and can be used by anyone with the desire to improve their life by setting and achieving goals. The SMART Goals method of goal setting works because it lays each step out for you. M is for measurable. By implementing the SMART Goals system, you will gain the ability to achieve your goals, faster and with a higher success rate.

THE POWER OF WRITING YOUR SMART GOALS DOWN AND REVIEWING THEM REGULARLY

Writing your goals down as you set them; will help your brain encode the plan, further solidifying your goal. The mere act of writing an idea down makes it more likely you will remember it. This is the reason college students take notes in lectures, note taking provides a much higher probability of remembering the information. Similarly, when you draft your goal in writing, you have a better chance of success. After writing out your goal, be sure to place it somewhere that you can see it easily. Places like on the fridge, on your phone, on a mirror, at your desk are all excellent areas, where you can easily visually access your goal. Seeing the words you wrote out serves as a reminder and as motivation to continue with your efforts.

SMART GOALS

S:

M:

A:

R:

T:

Not only will you be reminded of your goal by visually seeing the words written, but you should also take the time for an active review of your goal. Regularly, actively reviewing your written goal will increase your chances of success. An active review of your goal should include contemplating the reasons behind your motivation for the goal, and your "why." Thinking about the reasons you set the particular goal will boost your motivation by reminding you why the goal matters to you, why you set it and what you expect to gain from it. Reviewing your goal will aid in renewed purpose and incentive, ultimately bumping up your likelihood of success. Countless studies find that writing out your goals produces higher success rates. Placing the words you've written in an easily accessible spot and reviewing them often will also help ensure that you follow through with the SMART goals you set for yourself.

SPECIFIC IN SMART GOALS

In the next step, you'll answer the five questions that asked you for more information. Your goal will look something like this: "I will drink 8 glasses of lemon water every day - 2 glasses before breakfast, 2 glasses with lunch, and 2 glasses after the gym." That's what this goal is all about. It makes it clear what your expectations are for yourself and makes it easier for you to be held accountable.

This is another example of a goal that doesn't have a lot of specifics or focus. "I will exercise more." This goal is positive and relevant, but it doesn't say what it wants you to do. This makes it more likely that you'll fail. Answering the five w's will give you the specifics you need to set meaningful, constructive goals that are more likely to be achieved.

I'll sit, read and write in the journal "Write the Vision through Personal Development" by Mychosia Nightingale today for 45 minutes every morning before I start my business routine. People make plans all the time, but this one is very detailed. It says what, where, how, and when you're going to do it. Its specifics will make it more likely to achieve its goal than the first, more general statement.

As part of the acronym, SMART goals, the letter S stands for being very specific. People start by writing down their specific goals. This is the first step to making goals that last and are successful!

SET YOUR GOAL WITH INTENTION

Setting goals with the intention can help one to focus on what needs to be done and take effective measures towards achieving them. When setting goals, it is important to ensure that they are achievable and realistic. One should also ensure that the goal is measurable, so progress can be tracked against it. Furthermore, having clear objectives helps to provide motivation and a sense of purpose, as well as promote action orientation.

Creating measurable goals is an important step in any task or project, for it allows us to track our progress and chart our successes. Examples of goals can include increasing medical cannabis sales by 10%, reducing customer service wait times by 25%, or launching a new cannabis product within 6 months. Additionally, goals should have specific deadlines associated with them in order to encourage timely completion and maintain accountability.

Furthermore, when setting goals with the intention it is beneficial to break down the main objective into smaller tasks or milestones. This way it becomes easier to focus on individual tasks rather than feeling overwhelmed by the overall objective. Each task should be made manageable enough so that it can be completed within a reasonable period of time and eventually lead toward the end goal. Additionally, each milestone should have its own deadline in order for its completion date to remain visible at all times.

Lastly, one must ensure a positive outlook while setting their goals while also being proactive regarding their intentions instead of relying solely on luck or chance for success. Having a positive attitude during project planning helps keep individuals motivated over time towards seeing results even when facing challenges along the journey. It is also beneficial for review meetings allowing team members to stay focused on team dynamics and create a supportive environment where ideas are shared freely which ultimately boosts morale and leads to productivity overall.

BE SPECIFIC IN GOAL SETTING

As you write down your goals, you need to be very specific. Overly broad goals will make it hard to know where to go and how to focus on what's important. There are a lot of things that can go wrong if your goals are too broad. Suppose you want to drink more water each day. "I will drink more water every day." This is way too broad. You will be able to make excuses if you don't give specifics. In this case, the wording doesn't hold you to account; it isn't enough of a detailed plan for you to follow through with, either. Instead, explain the specifics.

Answering a few questions about your goal will help you figure out what you want and how to get there. Who? What? When? Where? Why? Answering these five questions will help you get more specific and motivated about your goal. Make a list of these five questions to help you write your goal.

Who will this goal involve?

____

____

What exactly do I want to accomplish?

____

____

____

When do I want to accomplish this goal?

____

Where will you achieve this goal?

____

____

MEASURABLE IN GOAL SETTING

The second part of the SMART Goals method is measuring your progress toward the goals you've set. If you don't have a way to tell if you're making progress toward your goal, you won't know. In order to keep going and stay motivated, you need to be able to see how far you've come. You can do this by celebrating the small milestones you reach as you go. In order to make it easier to see how far you've come, you'll need a set of criteria for measuring your progress. Similar to the Specific step used in SMART Goals, you will need to answer a few questions regarding your goal as a criterion for measuring progress data:

How many?
How much?
What is the indicator of progress?

How many or how much refers to progress as an indicator of what success for your specific goal looks like. The indicator of progress signifies the way in which you decide to track the progress you have made.

Using the same goal as above, to lose 10 pounds by exercising more. More specifically stated, "I will go to the gym to work out for 45 minutes every day weekday morning before work, in order to lose 2 pounds per week." Now not only is the goal specific and clearly stated, we have added the quantity of measurement for the goal, 2 pounds per week. In this case the indicator of measurement would be the scale. In the arena of business, an example might be, if the goal is, "I will build a cannabis brand awareness through social media, to increase gross profits by 20% per month." The quantity of measurement and the indicator is the profit increase in comparison to previous months.

Putting the SMART Goals method to use has proven to produce a higher success rate for goal achievement. Measuring your goals is an important part of this process. When you track your progress, you will have the ability to stay more motivated towards your goal and keep a stronger focus.

GOALS

WHEN SETTING GOALS, MAKE SURE IT FOLLOWS THE SMART STRUCTURE. USE THE QUESTIONS BELOW TO CREATE YOUR GOALS.

S	**SPECIFIC** WHAT DO I WANT TO ACCOMPLISH?	
M	**MEASURABLE** HOW WILL I KNOW WHEN IT IS ACCOMPLISHED?	
A	**ACHIEVABLE** HOW CAN THE GOAL BE ACCOMPLISHED?	
R	**RELEVANT** DOES THIS SEEM WORTHWHILE?	
T	**TIME BOUND** WHEN CAN I ACCOMPLISH THIS GOAL?	

MONTHLY GOALS #1

Goals:

Main GOAL for this month:

WEEKLY MINI GOALS :

Week 1:	Week 2:	Week 3:	Week 4:

Why this Goal is important to me:

How I will stay accountable:

MONTHLY GOALS #2

Goals:

Main GOAL for this month:

WEEKLY MINI GOALS

Week 1:	Week 2:	Week 3:	Week 4:

Why this Goal is important to me:

How I will stay accountable:

TRACKING PROGRESS GOAL#1

Goal: | Deadline:

STEP 1 → STEP 2 → STEP 3

↓

STEP 4 → STEP 5 → STEP 6

↓

STEP 7 → STEP 8 → STEP 9

↓

STEP 10

NOTES

TRACKING PROGRESS GOAL#2

Goal: Deadline:

STEP 1

STEP 2

STEP 3

STEP4

STEP5

STEP6

STEP7

STEP8

STEP9

STEP10

NOTES

ACHIEVABLE IN GOAL SETTING

The A, in SMART Goals, represents achievable. When setting goals, be sure to choose a goal that is achievable, means your goals should be within reasonable reach for you. Although the goals you set should stretch you out of your comfort zone and excite you, your goals should remain within reach. If a goal is impossible to achieve your efforts are futile. It becomes unproductive to put your time and energy toward a goal that will never come to fruition.

You will end up losing motivation and feel like giving up if you aren't able to succeed or celebrate your milestones along the way. Instead, be sure to set a goal that you can accomplish, this way you will keep focus and motivation, and have a chance of greater success. Along with your goal being unattainable, be sure that when you draft your goal, it's written in a way that allows you responsibility for your goal. You should state your goals in a way that gives you control over the outcome. No one other than you should be the subject of your goal. You should state attainable goals with success in mind.

Keep your goals challenging yet attainable and you will be on your way to being successful with your goals

For example, let's say you feel that you would benefit professionally from reading more books that pertain to your business. So, your goal might be, "I will read a business related book every night before bed for 20 minutes, with my goal to be to read one business book per month, for 6 months." This goal is attainable because what you're asking of yourself is reasonable and achievable. The goal also only involves one person, you, who follows through to ensure success.

Another way to assist attainable goals in being successful is through setting milestone goals. Milestone goals are small goals that you can set along the pathway to your goal. For example, in the instance above, a milestone goal could be to check in with yourself once a week. Checking in on your own accountability is a great way to stay on track. If you have followed through with your goal for the week, in this case, reading your business book for 20 minutes every evening, you will know you are making progress toward your goal. As we already know, tracking or measuring your progress helps secure a greater success rate for your goal.

MY ACHIEVABLE GOALS #1

Start date: ____________ Deadline: ____________

End date: ____________ Duration: ____________

GOAL

ACTION STEPS

- [ ] ____________
- [ ] ____________
- [ ] ____________
- [ ] ____________
- [ ] ____________
- [ ] ____________
- [ ] ____________
- [ ] ____________

AFFIRMATION

NOTES

MY ACHIEVABLE GOALS #2

Start date: ____________________ Deadline: ____________________

End date: ____________________ Duration: ____________________

GOAL

AFFIRMATION

ACTION STEPS

- [ ] ____________________
- [ ] ____________________
- [ ] ____________________
- [ ] ____________________
- [ ] ____________________
- [ ] ____________________
- [ ] ____________________
- [ ] ____________________

NOTES

RELEVANCY IN GOAL SETTING

In goal setting, "your why" refers to how important a goal is to you. The "R" stands for "relevant" in the SMART Goals method of goal setting. This part of setting a goal for yourself is important because it makes sure the goal is important to you. Trying to reach a goal that doesn't really bother you doesn't make sense. Goals should make us move forward toward something important. If your goal is important, it should also work well with your other plans in life.

So, how do you figure out whether or not something you want to do is important? By decide the relevance of a goal by answering a few questions pertaining to the goal and your current life. Questions like:

Does this goal seem worthwhile? Is the tradeoff of time and effort worth the result?

____

____

Does it align well with my other efforts and goals? Are other aspects of your life driving forward in the same direction?

____

____

Is this the right time for this goal? Does this goal fit in with your personal goals? Does it make sense financially?

____

____

Am I the right person for this goal? Is this goal attainable? Do I have the skills and ability for success in the goal?

____

____

Coming up with answers to these questions will help you determine the goal's relevance in your life. Some of these questions are not necessarily straightforward, black and white. You will need to dig deep to answer some of these questions to find the real "why" of your desired goal, to know if it's relevant enough to move forward.

An example of a goal relevant to one's life might be for someone whose goal is to be promoted in their field, to take available online courses, to gain knowledge and experience of their desired position. This plan is worthwhile because it provides professional experience. They offer the courses online, so you can take them at a time convenient for the subject. Online courses are affordable, so most likely they will make financial sense. The online courses will ultimately propel the subject forward, toward an even bigger goal, the eventual promotion.

Relevance of a goal is an important part of goal setting. Deciding if a goal is relevant helps you match your goals to the rest of your life, helps you know if the goal matters to you, and if the time is the right time to achieve the goal. Sometimes, one must truly examine themselves and their life to determine relevance of a desired goal.

Reach your goals by writing them down part of your daily routine. Do it now. Make it habit.

TIMELY IN SMART GOAL

A good way to help yourself keep moving forward is by setting goals for what comes next. For example, if you've been dragging your feet about cleaning out your closet, setting a goal for getting it done will motivate you to get started. In addition, it will give you a clear timeline for when you'll be finished with the task: if you set a deadline for 1 week from today, it will give you something concrete to be working toward and remind you that this is something that needs to be done sooner rather than later.

You can put in your deadlines for each project, then schedule the time during which you want to work on them. When setting appointments in your calendar, choose times that are realistic for your needs. For instance, if you have to submit your paper by the end of the week, but it's already Friday and you haven't had any time yet to work on it, set an appointment for the next morning or afternoon. That way, if anything comes up and you don't have enough time in the morning or afternoon, well—it was already in your calendar so there's no need to worry about forgetting.

In addition to helping keep momentum going in the right direction, goals also give us something to work toward. When we're working toward a specific end point or event in the future

HOW TO PRIORITIZE YOUR TASK & TIME MANGEMENT

1. Identify Your Goals:

Take some time to think about your long-term goals and what you want to achieve in life. This will help you prioritize tasks and set yourself up for success.

2. Create a To-Do List:

List out all the tasks that need to be completed, including small and large tasks. Make sure to prioritize the most important tasks first, as they will have the most impact on your personal development.

3. Schedule Time:

Schedule time for yourself each day to work on personal development tasks. This will help you stay organized and focused on the tasks that need to be completed.

4. Set Deadlines:

Set deadlines for yourself to help stay motivated and on track. This will also help you to better prioritize your tasks and stay organized.

5. Take Breaks:

Make sure to take breaks throughout the day. This will help you stay focused and productive.

6. Track Your Progress:

Track your progress to stay motivated and on track with your goals. This will also help you to see what tasks have been completed and what still needs to be done.

7. Ask For Help:

Don't be afraid to ask for help if needed. This will help you stay on track and focused on your goals.

8. Reward Yourself:

Reward yourself for completing tasks and reaching goals. This will help you stay motivated and on track.

GOAL TIMELINE

TIMELINE	WHAT / VISION	HOW?
3 Month		Done ☐
6 Month		Done ☐
1 year		Done ☐
2 Years		Done ☐
3 years		Done ☐

Let's Do the Work Questionaire

BELIEVE	Setting small achievable goals, developing positive self-talk, engaging in activities that build self-confidence, and using positive affirmations can all help you believe in yourself.	BELIEVE
AREAS	Areas you can focus on developing strong communication skills, developing emotional intelligence, improving problem-solving skills, and learning to manage stress and anxiety.	AREAS
STEPS	To achieve these goals, you can take steps such as: setting specific, achievable goals; actively participating in activities and classes that challenge you; engaging in self-reflection and journaling; reading books and articles related to the topics; developing a positive and constructive attitude; and engaging in meaningful conversations with others.	STEPS

BELIEVE

IDENTIFY WAYS YOU CAN BELIEVE IN YOURSELF.

BELIEVE

AREAS

WHAT SPECIFIC AREAS OF PERSONAL GROWTH DO YOU WANT TO FOCUS ON?

AREAS

STEPS

WHAT STEPS WILL YOU TAKE TO ACHIEVE THESE GOALS?

STEPS

SPECIFIC

Goals can be achieved with help from mentors, coaches, and other professionals who can provide guidance and support. They can help set realistic goals, create plans to reach them, and hold you accountable.

SPECIFIC

AMOUNT

The goal depends on the amount of time you have available in your schedule look to focus on time managment.

AMOUNT

RESULTS

The results we can achieve depend on our goals and the effort we put in.

RESULTS

SPECIFIC

SPECIFIC GOALS, PEOPLE WHO CAN HELP YOU ACHIEVE THEM

SPECIFIC

AMOUNT

THE AMOUNT OF TIME YOU'RE INVESTING IN EACH GOAL

AMOUNT

RESULTS

RESULTS YOU'VE ACHIEVED

RESULTS

AUTHENTIC

Be true to yourself and your values. Set realistic goals and take action to achieve them. Be open to feedback and criticism and use it to improve yourself. Embrace your strengths and weaknesses and use them to your advantage. Show kindness and respect to others and be open to different perspectives.

AUTHENTIC

LEVEL UP

Level up by setting personal goals and actively striving to achieve them. Use positive reinforcement, such as rewarding yourself with something special when you reach a milestone, to motivate and encourage yourself. Additionally, take every opportunity to learn something new and practice the skills you need to improve.

LEVEL UP

TRUTH

Live your truth by being honest with yourself and others, standing up for what you believe in, and taking responsibility for your actions.

AUTHENTIC

HOW CAN YOU BE AUTHENTIC TO YOURSELF AND GOALS?

AUTHENTIC

LEVEL UP

WILL YOU FORCE YOURSELF TO LEVEL UP AND HOW?

LEVEL UP

TRUTH

ARE YOU GOING TO LIVE YOUR TRUTH & HOW?

TRUTH

VISION	Create an action plan that clearly outlines your growth and objectives, and set achievable milestones that will help you reach them. From there, you will need to focus on consistency and dedication in order to stay on track.	VISION
FAILURES	Taking responsibility for your actions, learning from your mistakes, and having a positive attitude. I would also focus on setting achievable goals and trying to stay motivated. Additionally, seek help and advice from mentors and other trusted individuals who can provide guidance and support.	FAILURES
PATH	See your life by setting goals and taking action to achieve them. Additionally, staying focused, having a positive attitude, staying organized, and being open to new ideas and experiences can help you create the life you want.	PATH

VISION

VISION

EXECUTE YOUR VISION YOU HAVE FOR YOURSELF

FAILURES

FAILURES

HOW WILL YOU OVERCOME YOUR FAILURES?

PATH

PATH

HAVE YOU CHOSEN THE PATH YOU DESIRE TO SEE YOUR LIFE? EXPLAIN

GREATNESS

Greatness to me looks like living a life of purpose, making a positive impact on the world, and striving to continuously improve oneself. believe you are close to it in your growth, as you are continually pushing yourself to reach higher and make a difference.

GREATNESS

ADVERSITY

You will face many adversities throughout your life, but the most significant was overcoming and learning the power of discipline. it can teach you resilience, determination, and the power of hard work. It also taught me the importance of embracing failure and using it as a learning opportunity.

ADVERSITY

PATIENCE

WHAT LEVEL OF PATIENCE DO YOU HAVE FOR YOURSELF TO WORK ON YOURSELF?

PATIENCE

GREATNESS

WHATS DOES GREATNESS LOOK LIKE FOR YOU?
ARE YOU CLOSE TO IT IN YOUR GROWTH?

GREATNESS

ADVERSITY

WHAT ADVERSITY HAVE YOU FACE & HOW
DID IT CHANGE YOU?

ADVERSITY

PATIENCE

WHAT LEVEL OF PATIENCE DO YOU HAVE
FOR YOURSELF TO WORK ON YOURSELF?

PATIENCE

DEVELOP CONFIDENCE

CONFIDENCE	Believe in yourself, believe that you can do it, and trust your own abilities. Take risks. Don't be afraid to take risks and try new things. This will help you gain confidence in yourself and your abilities. Practice positive self-talk. Talk to yourself in a positive way and focus on your strengths. Celebrate your successes. Celebrate your successes, no matter how small they may be. This will give you the motivation to keep going and will help boost your confidence. Face your fears. Facing your fears can help you become more confident. Don't be afraid to step out of your comfort zone and try things that may be difficult. Surround yourself with positive people. Spend time with people who are positive and supportive. This will help create a positive environment and make it easier to stay motivated. Be flexible. Be open to change and don't be afraid to take on new challenges. This will help you develop confidence in your ability to adapt and handle new situations.	CONFIDENCE
ABILITIES	Developing confidence in your abilities is a process that involves setting realistic goals, celebrating small successes, and pushing yourself outside of your comfort zone. It also involves reframing negative thoughts and surrounding yourself with supportive people.	ABILITIES
FORGIVENESS	Mentors and accountability partners can be invaluable resources when it comes to achieving success. Mentors can provide guidance and support, while accountability partners can help keep you on track and motivate you to reach your goals. Having both is a great way to stay motivated and focused on achieving success.	FORGIVENESS

DEVELOP CONFIDENCE

CONFIDENCE

CONFIDENCE

DEVELOP CONFIDENCE IN YOUR ABILITES

ABILITIES

ABILITIES

DO YOU HAVE MENTORS TO WORK WITH AND A ACCOUNTABILITY PARTNERS?

FORGIVENESS

FORGIVENESS

REGRETS

Understand how difficult it can be to let go of regrets, but it is important to recognize that we cannot change the past and that we must focus on the present moment. One way to start letting go of regrets is to practice self-compassion and acceptance. Remind yourself of all the positive qualities you possess and focus on the lessons learned from your regrets. Additionally, try to think about how you can use the regret as a learning experience to make better decisions in the future.

REGRETS

HAPPINESS

Spending quality time with loved ones, engaging in meaningful activities, taking care of your physical and mental health, and finding joy in everyday moments are all great ways to make yourself happy.

HAPPINESS

HARD TIMES

You will experience hard times and will embrace them as opportunities to learn and grow. just focused on the lessons you have learned and used them to inform your decisions going forward.

HARD TIMES

FOCUS ON REGRETS YOU ARE NOT ABLE TO LET GO, FIND WAYS TO LET GO.

REGRETS

REGRETS

ARE YOU HAPPY? IF NOT FOCUS ON WAYS THAT CAN MAKE YOU HAPPY

HAPPINESS

HAPPINESS

HAVE YOU EXPERIENCED ANY HARD TIMES, EMBRACE IT AND FOCUS ON THE LESSON FROM IT

HARD TIMES

HARD TIMES

ARE YOU A HUMBLE PERSON?

HUMBLENESS

- Take time to really hear what other people have to say.
- Acknowledge your mistakes. Admit when you are wrong and apologize sincerely.
- Be kind. Treat others with respect, even when there are disagreements.
- Ask for help. Don't be afraid to reach out to others for assistance.
- Be grateful. Express your appreciation for the help or support you receive.
- Speak humbly. Avoid boasting about your accomplishments and be humble about your successes.
- Help others. Look for ways to lend a hand to those who need it.
- Forgive. Let go of grudges and learn to forgive those who have wronged you.
- Practice humility. Focus on what you can learn rather than what you already know.
- Show humility. Avoid comparing yourself to others and practice humility in all areas of your life.

HUMBLENESS

HUMBLENESS

You can practice humility when interacting with others by being open to feedback, being willing to acknowledge mistakes, and being gracious when receiving compliments or praise.

HUMBLENESS

CRITICISM

Staying humble in the face of criticism is key to personal growth. It is important to listen to what is being said, reflect on it, and assess the validity of the criticism. Taking a step back and objectively analyzing the feedback, will help to put things into perspective and identify areas of improvement. This can be done by keeping an open mind, being willing to learn, and actively engaging in self-evaluation and self-improvement.

CRITICISM

HUMBLENESS

ARE YOU A HUMBLE PERSON?

HUMBLENESS

HUMBLENESS

HOW CAN YOU PRACTICE HUMILITY WHEN INTERACTING WITH OTHERS TO BENEFIT YOU?

HUMBLENESS

CRITICISM

HOW CAN YOU STAY HUMBLE IN THE FACE OF CRITICISM? KEEP IN MIND GROWTH

CRITICISM

INSIDE	Unleash and share your gifts, start by taking time to get to know yourself, explore your interests and passions, and find creative ways to express them. Make sure to stay open to learning new things and allowing yourself to grow. Find a supportive community to share your gifts with and be vulnerable with.
CHEATING	Cutting corners is not a good idea as it often results in a lower quality product or service, and can ultimately hurt you more than it helps you. Instead, focus on finding ways to streamline processes and increase efficiency. This will help you achieve your goals without compromising on quality.
FEAR	Being honest and having the courage to face difficult situations is the key to living a life of integrity and purpose.

INSIDE

CREATE WHAT'S INSIDE OF YOU UNLEASH IT, SHARE YOUR GIFTS

INSIDE

CHEATING

DO YOU CUT CORNERS, HOW DID THAT HELP YOU, NOTE ITS HURTS YOU MORE THAN HELP YOU

CHEATING

FEAR

DO YOU OPERATE IN FEAR? WHY BE HONEST

FEAR

EGO

I allowed my ego to overcome me when I refused to collaborate with my team on this certain project. I was so sure of my own ideas that I refused to hear any other suggestions and ended up with a subpar outcome. Ultimately, I didn't get anything out of it other than embarrassment when my team pointed out that my version was inferior to the team's final version. Never allow ego to take over be humble and listen.

EGO

ADVANCE

Focus on developing your skills and knowledge, set goals, and take action to achieve them. Additionally, be honest with yourself and others about what you know and can do, and be open to feedback and criticism.

ADVANCE

EMPOWERMENT

Asking yourself empowering questions can help you to overcome any challenge and become more self-confident.

1. What have I achieved today that I am proud of?
2. What can I do today to bring me one step closer to my goals?
3. What is one thing I can do today to make myself happier?
4. What can I do to take better care of myself?
5. What would I do if I knew I could not fail?

EMPOWERMENT

EGO

DO YOU HAVE A BIG EGO? WRITE A TIME YOU ALLOWED YOUR EGO TO OVERCOME YOU. WHAT DID YOU GET OUT OF IT? EGOS CAN ONLY HURT YOU

EGO

ADVANCE

WAYS TO ADVANCE YOURSELF, BE HONEST

ADVANCE

EMPOWERMENT

ASK YOURSELF EMPOWERING QUESTIONS ?

EMPOWERMENT

LISTENING

Focus on understanding the other person's point of view by engaging in open-ended questions, making eye contact, avoiding distractions, and repeating back what you heard to ensure understanding.

LISTENING

EVOLVE

Set short-term and long-term goals, create action plans to achieve them, and hold yourself accountable. Additionally, continually challenge yourself to learn new things and take risks to reach your goals. Lastly, take time to reflect on your progress and adjust your plans as needed.

EVOLVE

VIBRATION

Focus on positive thoughts and feelings. Make an effort to consciously redirect your thoughts towards more positive and uplifting ideas. It can also help to practice positive affirmations, gratitude, and self-care. Additionally, engaging in activities that bring joy and pleasure can help to raise your vibration and create a more positive outlook.?

VIBRATION

LISTENING

HAVE YOU MASTERED THE ART OF ACTIVE LISTENING TO UNDERSTAND THE PERSON'S POINT OF VIEW ?

LISTENING

EVOLVE

ARE YOU CONSISTENTLY EVOLVING IN YOUR GOALS/LIFE?

EVOLVE

VIBRATION

ARE YOU SHIFTING YOUR VIBRATION? HOW ?

VIBRATION

DESIRE

To see desire, dedication, and discipline in your life and goals, focus on setting clear objectives and creating actionable steps to reach them. Focus on the process of achieving your goals, not just the end result, and stay consistent and motivated. Monitor your progress, and reward yourself for the small successes along the way. Stay disciplined and do not give up in the face of challenges.

BEST

Focus on the present and prioritize self-care. Set realistic goals and create a plan to reach them. Celebrate small successes, stay organized, and practice mindfulness and gratitude. Take time to relax and find a balance between work and leisure. Spend time with those who love and support you, and don't be afraid to ask for help when needed.

LEVERAGING

Leveraging negativity in your life and goals can help you stay motivated and focused. By acknowledging and understanding the negative, you can better understand the obstacles you will face and create strategies to overcome them. You can also use the negative to reframe it as a learning experience and use it to gain insight into how to achieve your goals.

DO YOU SEE DESIRE, DEDICATION, AND DISCIPLINE IN YOUR LIFE, GOALS AND MORE?

DESIRE

DESIRE

ARE YOU DISPLAYING YOUR BEST IN THIS CURRENT MOMENT OF YOUR LIFE?

BEST

BEST

ARE YOU LEVERAGING NEGATIVITY IN YOUR LIFE/GOALS IN YOUR LIFE?

LEVERAGING

LEVERAGING

STRUGGLES

Turn your struggles into strength, and focus on developing resilience, self-compassion, and problem-solving skills. Seek out support from friends and family, practice positive self-talk, and make time for self-care. Set goals and take small steps each day to help you move forward.

STRUGGLES

MASTER

Start by taking small steps and gradually working your way up to bigger challenges. Set realistic goals and practice positive self-talk to help build your confidence as you go. Additionally, seek out support from trusted friends and family to help you stay motivated and build resilience.

MASTER

VISION

Try to focus and work on your vision at least weekly. use the time to review your vision and consider any changes needed to be made. also, use the time to brainstorm ideas and plan actions to help yourself move closer to achieving your vision.

VISION

ARE YOU TURNING YOUR STRUGGLES INTO STRENGTH IF SO HOW ?

STRUGGLES

STRUGGLES

HAVE YOU MASTERED HOW TO FUNCTION OUTSIDE OF YOUR COMFORT ZONE?

MASTER

MASTER

VISION, HOW OFTEN DO YOU FOCUS & WORK ON YOUR VISION?

VISION

VISION

EFFECTIVENESS

The best way to be effective in life with your goals and vision is to set realistic, achievable goals, create a plan of action to reach those goals, and take consistent, dedicated action towards achieving them.

EFFECTIVENESS

DEVELOP

The best way to develop beneficial relationships around yourself is to be kind and open, show a genuine interest in those you interact with, and work to build trust and mutual respect.

DEVELOP

TAPPING

Exploring new activities and interests, taking time to relax and daydream, using brainstorming and mind mapping, and trying out different creative outlets such as art, music, writing, photography, and more.

ARE YOU BEING EFFECTIVE IN YOUR LIFE WITH YOUR GOALS/VISION ?

EFFECTIVENESS

EFFECTIVENESS

ARE YOU DEVELOPING BENEFICIAL RELATIONSHIPS AROUND YOURSELF?

DEVELOP

DEVELOP

ARE YOU TAPPING INTO YOUR CREATIVITY?

TAPPING

TAPPING

MINDSET

Create a positive mindset by focusing on gratitude, setting goals, practicing self-care, and connecting with your family and friends.

GRATITUDE

To display gratitude in your life, make a point to recognize the things that you are thankful for and express your appreciation to those around you. Find ways to show your gratitude, such as writing thank you notes, saying kind words to those you care about, volunteering your time, or showing acts of kindness.

VALUE

Adding value to your surroundings starts with finding ways to contribute to the betterment of the people and environment around you. This can be done through volunteer work, engaging in meaningful conversations, and being an active listener. Additionally, by being kind and respectful to others, you can create a positive atmosphere and make a lasting impact.

WHAT MINDSET DO YOU HAVE THAT IS BENEFICIAL TO YOU AND YOUR FAMILY?

MINDSET

MINDSET

ARE YOU DISPLAYING GRATITUDE IN YOUR LIFE? HOW?

GRATITUDE

GRATITUDE

ARE YOU ADDING VALUE TO YOUR SURROUNDINGS? HOW?

VALUE

VALUE

PUSH

Focus on setting and achieving challenging goals, staying motivated and committed, and continually learning and improving. Additionally, it can be helpful to track your progress, seek feedback from others, and set up systems for accountability and support.

PUSH

POTENTIAL

To outwork the potential you, focus on setting goals and taking actionable steps to reach them. Track your progress, stay motivated, and challenge yourself to go beyond what you think you're capable of.

POTENTIAL

THINKER

Focus on making decisions that will have a positive impact in the long run and consider the potential consequences of those decisions. Set long-term goals and break them down into achievable short-term objectives. Also, avoid taking shortcuts or making decisions based on immediate gratification.

THINKER

ARE YOU PUSHING YOURSELF TO THE NEXT LEVEL IF SO, HOW EFFECTIVE ARE YOU?

PUSH

PUSH

YOU VS YOU, ARE YOU OUTWORKING THE POTENTIAL YOU?

POTENTIAL

POTENTIAL

ARE YOU A LONG TERM THINKER?

THINKER

THINKER

CHALLENGE

Challenge yourself by setting goals and striving to reach them, engaging in regular self-reflection and self-improvement, and taking on new challenges and opportunities that will help you learn and develop new skills.

CHALLENGE

PROTECTING

Protecting your dreams/visions/goals by setting realistic and achievable goals, staying focused, and taking consistent action.

PROTECTING

DEFINE

Defining who you are and what you want in life is an ongoing process of self-reflection and exploration. Strive to continually learn more about yourself, your values, and your goals, and to use that knowledge to direct your decisions and actions. Monitor yourself daily to track your progress through journaling. revise or change anything along the way if needed.

DEFINE

CHALLENGE

ARE YOU CHALLENGING YOUR GROWTH? IF SO HOW ?

CHALLENGE

PROTECTING

ARE YOU PROTECTING YOUR DREAMS/VISIONS/GOALS? HOW?

PROTECTING

DEFINE

DEFINE OUT WHO YOU ARE AND WHAT YOU WANT IN LIFE?

DEFINE

CHARACTER

Building your character involves developing traits that make you unique and stand out from the crowd. To do this, you should focus on self-reflection, self-improvement, and self-discipline. Set goals for yourself, challenge yourself to do better and practice the values that you want to embody. Additionally, focus on building relationships with those around you and practice gratitude and kindness.

CHARACTER

REPUTATION

Creating principles, guidelines, and organization in your life starts with setting goals and developing a plan to achieve them. Your character, your word, and more are based on the system you stay loyal to for yourself and others. This plan should include breaking down large tasks into smaller steps and assigning deadlines for each step. Its important to create a system to track progress and adjust the plan if needed.

REPUTATION

HONESTY

Be authentic, be transparent, and be true to yourself and to others. Maintain an attitude of integrity in your life and strive to always do the right thing. Respect yourself and others, and be honest in all your dealings. Always finish what you start.

CHARACTER

HOW ARE YOU BUILDING YOUR CHARACTER?

CHARACTER

REPUTATION

ARE CREATING YOUR PRNICPLES, GUIDELINES AND ORGANIZATION IN YOUR LIFE?

REPUTATION

HONESTY

ARE YOU AN UPRIGHT PERSON AND HONEST WITH YOURSELF AND OTHERS AT ALL TIMES?

HONESTY

SILENCE

Create a plan in silence for how you will reach your goal, including the timeline and resources. Be consistent. Sticking to your plan is essential for achieving your goal. Take consistent, small steps every day to make progress. Don't compare yourself to others. Everyone's journey is different, so stay focused on your own progress. Don't be afraid to ask for help. Reach out to people you trust and respect for advice and support. Embrace failure. Mistakes and setbacks are part of the learning process. Learn from them and keep going. Celebrate your successes. Don't forget to celebrate the small victories along the way. They will help keep you motivated.

SILENCE

INTEGRITY

Start by being a person of integrity yourself. People of integrity tend to be attracted to and seek out, others with the same values. Look for people who are honest and dependable. Notice how they handle themselves in different situations, and how they interact with others. Get to know people in your community and network. Look for people who share your values and who are respected by their peers. Make it a point to spend time with people who have integrity. Join groups or activities that attract individuals who place a high value on honesty and accountability. Speak up when you witness someone cheating or taking advantage of someone else. People of integrity are often willing to stand up for what's right, even if it's unpopular. Be patient. It takes time to build strong relationships with people who have integrity. Put in the effort and you'll find that it's worth it.

INTEGRITY

CALMNESS

Take a deep breath. Taking a few deep breaths can be a great way to calm your mind and body. Deep breathing helps to reduce tension and stress in the body and can help bring a sense of peace and relaxation. Meditate. Meditation is an ancient practice that has been used for centuries to help people find inner peace and calmness. It can be done anywhere and requires no special equipment.

Exercise. Exercise can be a great way to reduce stress and release tension in the body. As an added bonus, it can also help to improve your mood and mental clarity.

Practice mindfulness. Mindfulness is the practice of being present at the moment and acknowledging your thoughts and feelings without judgment. Practicing mindfulness can help to cultivate a sense of calmness and peace.

CALMNESS

SILENCE

ARE YOU BUILDING IN SILENCE?

SILENCE

INTEGRITY

ARE YOU SURROUNDING YOURSELF WITH PEOPLE OF INTEGRITY?

INTEGRITY

CALMNESS

ARE YOU PRACTICING CALMNESS?

CALMNESS

COMPLAIN

If you are feeling the urge to complain, try to first take a step back and identify the root cause of the problem. Once you have identified the problem, brainstorm possible solutions and pick the one that best fits your situation. If the problem is out of your control, find a healthy and productive way to manage your emotions and find a positive perspective.

COMPLAIN

CHANGE

Acknowledge the change: Recognize the change and accept its presence in your life.
Reflect on the situation: Consider why the change is occurring, what it means for you, and how it is impacting your life.
Set goals: Take some time to think about how you want to move forward. What are your goals for the future?
Take action: Take small steps towards achieving your goals. Focus on what you can do today to make progress.
Stay positive: Remember that change can be positive and can bring new opportunities. Look for the silver lining in the situation.
Seek support: Talk to friends or family members if you need help or just want to vent. Seek professional help if needed.
Learn from the experience: Reflect on the experience and consider what lessons you can take away.

CHANGE

THOUGHTS

Practice Mindfulness: Mindfulness is being aware and present in the moment. This can help you to stay focused on the present moment and observe thoughts and feelings without judgment.
Challenge Negative Thoughts: When negative thoughts pop up, take a moment to challenge them. Ask yourself if this thought is helpful or if it is based on facts. If not, replace it with a more positive view.
Change Your Focus: When you find yourself ruminating on negative thoughts or worries, try to focus on something else. This could be a physical activity, like going for a walk or doing some yoga, or something creative like drawing or writing.
Talk to Someone: Talking to a supportive friend or family member can help to get things off your chest and provide you with a different perspective.
Practice Self-Care: Taking time for yourself and doing things that make you feel good can help to reduce stress and create positive thinking patterns. Consider activities such as meditation, journaling, playing music, or reading a book.

THOUGHTS

COMPLAIN

NEVER COMPLAIN FIGURE OUT A WAY TO FIX IT

COMPLAIN

CHANGE

EMBRACE THE CHANGE IN YOUR LIFE

CHANGE

THOUGHTS

ARE YOU MANAGING YOUR THOUGHTS?

THOUGHTS

ARE YOU ENVIOUS OR JEALOUS

ENVIOUS	Acknowledge your feelings. It's important to recognize that feeling jealous or envious is normal, and it doesn't make you a bad person. Identify the source of your envy. When you're feeling envious of someone, take a step back and try to identify what it is that you're actually feeling envious of. Celebrate other people's successes. Instead of feeling jealous or envious, try to focus on celebrating other people's success. Acknowledge their hard work and find joy in their accomplishments. Focus on yourself. Instead of comparing yourself to others, focus on your own goals and progress. Celebrate your successes and take steps to reach your goals. How that comparison is the thief of joy. Instead of comparing yourself to others, remember that comparison is the thief of joy. Focus on your own journey and don't worry about what other people are doing.
STUDY	1. The 7 Habits of Highly Effective People by Stephen R. Covey 2. Think and Grow Rich by Napoleon Hill 3. How to Win Friends and Influence People by Dale Carnegie 4. The Power of Positive Thinking by Norman Vincent Peale 5. The Magic of Thinking Big by David J. Schwartz 6. Write the Vision by Mychosia Nightingale 7. 21 Keys of Success by Freeway Ricky Ross 8. The Power of Now by Eckhart Tolle 9. Rich Girl Code by Christia'n Annice 10. Shared Success Blueprint by Tiffany Gaines
EXPECTATIONS	Make a list of your goals and set a timeline for achieving them. Take actionable steps to reach your goals. Break down big goals into smaller, manageable tasks and focus on one at a time. Develop a growth mindset. Believe that you can learn and improve with hard work, dedication, and resilience. Monitor your progress and be honest about your progress. Celebrate and reward yourself for achieving your goals. Ask for feedback and use it to improve. Set new goals and challenge yourself. Learn from your mistakes and failures. Don't be afraid to take risks. Surround yourself with inspiring people and positive role models. Believe in yourself and your capabilities.

ENVIOUS

ARE YOU ENVIOUS OR JEALOUS

ENVIOUS

STUDY

WHAT ARE YOU STUDYING FOR THE IMPROVEMENT OF PERSONAL GROWTH?

STUDY

EXPECTATIONS

ARE YOU SETTING HIGH EXPECTATIONS FOR YOURSELF TO IMPROVE SELF?

EXPECTATIONS

Personal Goals

IDENTIFY YOUR TOP THREE PERSONAL GROWTH GOALS TO WORK ON? BE HONEST

WHAT SPECIFIC AREAS OF PERSONAL GROWTH DO YOU WANT TO FOCUS ON?

WHAT STEPS WILL YOU TAKE TO ACHIEVE THESE GOALS?

SPECIFIC GOALS, PEOPLE WHO CAN HELP YOU ACHIEVE THEM

THE AMOUNT OF TIME YOU'RE INVESTING IN EACH GOAL

RESULTS YOU'VE ACHIEVED

SHORT TERM GOAL

LONG TERM GOAL

OTHER GOALS

WEEKLY PLANNER

MONDAY	TUESDAY
WEDNESDAY	THURSDAY
FRIDAY	SATURDAY
SUNDAY	*notes*

Weekly Work Activity Plan #1

M

T

W

T

F

Daily Activities Tracker #1

6 Am

7 Am

8 Am

9 Am

10 Am

11 Am

12 Pm

1 Pm

2 Pm

3 Pm

4 Pm

5 Pm

6 Pm

REFLECTION #1

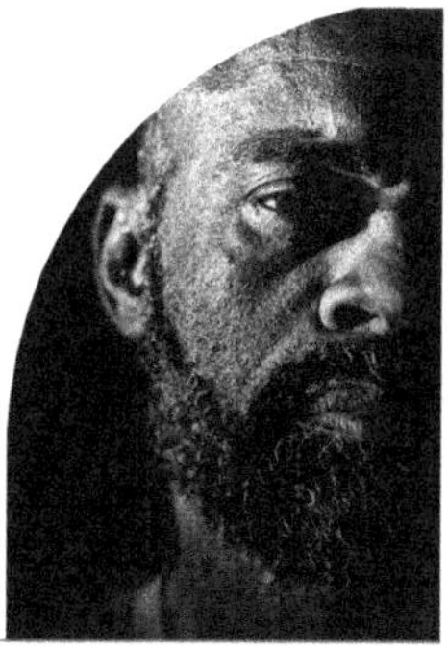

To grow, one must be accountable, going back to look at our mistakes and correct them.

IDENTIFY YOUR TOP THREE PERSONAL GROWTH GOALS TO WORK ON?

WHAT SPECIFIC AREAS OF PERSONAL GROWTH DO YOU WANT TO FOCUS ON?

WHAT STEPS WILL YOU TAKE TO ACHIEVE THESE GOALS?

SPECIFIC GOALS, PEOPLE WHO CAN HELP YOU ACHIEVE THEM

THE AMOUNT OF TIME YOU'RE INVESTING IN EACH GOAL

RESULTS YOU'VE ACHIEVED

SHORT TERM GOAL

LONG TERM GOAL

OTHER GOALS

WEEKLY PLANNER

MONDAY	TUESDAY
WEDNESDAY	THURSDAY
FRIDAY	SATURDAY
SUNDAY	*notes*

Weekly Work Activity Plan #2

M

T

W

T

F

Daily Activities Tracker #2

6 Am

7 Am

8 Am

9 Am

10 Am

11 Am

12 Pm

1 Pm

2 Pm

3 Pm

4 Pm

5 Pm

6 Pm

REFLECTION #2

To grow, one must be accountable, going back to look at our mistakes and correct them.

chapter six

EMPOWER YOUR GOALS

EMPOWER YOUR GOALS

Emotion is a powerful motivator for achieving your goals more quickly. Everything is determined by how you feel about your goals, so you must set goals that truly excite you, motivate you, and stretch your life. When you've identified your "Big Why" for each of your goals, those goals gain more clout, allowing you to achieve them more easily. Drilling down on your larger goals to find the "Big Why" enables you to determine whether they are essential to you or simply being used to help you avoid dealing with something you don't want to deal with.

1. Break your goal down into achievable steps. Take the time to plan out each step and set deadlines to complete them. Set yourself up for success by creating a positive and supportive environment, both mentally and physically. Identify and remove any distractions or barriers that could prevent you from achieving your goals. Celebrate your victories, no matter how small. Surround yourself with people who are supportive and encouraging. Find an accountability partner or mentor to help you stay on track. Visualize your success and allow yourself to feel the motivation and sense of accomplishment that comes with it. Look for new ways to challenge yourself and strive for excellence. Believe in yourself and your ability to reach your goals. Reward yourself for your hard work and dedication.

Once you've decided what you genuinely want, you'll begin to set high-level objectives. You'll combine several closely related goals into a single, new focused goal. The new focused goal will include powerful motivation. A motivation goal is simply one that piques your interest and that you are determined to achieve.

MOTIVATE YOUR GOALS

Motivation and the "Big Why" are very related in that they both help you find and use strong emotions as a way to reach your goals. To find your "Big Why," you must drill down to the specifics of your goals. Then you must make a motivation to help achieve your goals. This step in setting your goals is all about combining your list of goals that you came up with during your brainstorming sessions in Chapter 3. You can group goals that are similar together or goals that can support each other. It's essential to ensure that at least one of these goals is very important to you and has a lot of desire or emotional motivation. The desire to go on more trips might be a goal for you. Having more free time and making more money in a job you love could be two of your goals. These can all be combined into one simple, more powerful motivation goal.

SEPARATE GOALS

- Travel more
- Have more free time
- Make more money
- Work in a job you love

COMBINE YOUR SEPARATE GOALS TO CREATE MOTIVATION THAT EMPOWERS YOU

I will find a new hustle that I love, that will pay me more than [x amount] each month, and that will give me more free time so that I can travel as much as I want. The separate goals that are similar have been combined into a single goal, with a motivation. The motivation is the sincere desire to travel more, linked to the other three goals.

Motivation is essential for each of your goals. They make your goals stronger, more powerful, and a lot more excited. They become inspiring goals that can make you feel spirited. Goals that make you excited and make you want to act are what you want to work on. Your combined goals may be causing you to realize that some parts of them are only possible if other parts of the target are also done first. Changing and reordering your goals later isn't something you need to worry about. You can do that if you don't think they're being used in the right way for your current needs. It's also possible that your priorities might change over time, and you might no longer be as excited about some parts of your combined goals. That's fine, too. As a result, you can change your direction and change your combined goals to meet your needs if you want.

When you alter your combined goals, it's crucial to be completely honest with yourself. You must decide whether to alter your course or make an effort to be more truthful with yourself because you are beginning to doubt yourself. You're letting self-limiting ideas stand in the way of your goals if you decide to adjust them because you don't believe you can accomplish them. We shall discover how to use mind-programming techniques to alter these restricting ideas in the following chapter. Your development may be significantly slowed if you frequently modify your goals. Be constant and persevere in your efforts to set high-motivational goals.

PRACTICE MORE GRATITUDE

One of the most effective methods for achieving your goals is to practice gratitude. If you're feeling like you're not going to reach your goal, take a moment to think about what your life would be like if you had already achieved it. Imagine how much better it would be than where you are now. Then appreciate all of the things that are great about your current situation and how lucky you are to already have them. By focusing on the good aspects of your life, you'll not only feel better, but your brain will also produce positive neurotransmitters that help you reach your goal.

It sounds counter-intuitive: how is thinking about what you don't have going to help you get what you want? It's simple, really. Gratitude will help you focus on what's already good in your life and keep it that way. When you give thanks for all the good aspects of your life and the people who are a part of it, it's going to make it easier for you to keep those things in your life, not to mention come up with more good ideas for making and keeping new positive changes in your life. Our environment will start to reflect our thoughts and emotions as they change. This happens in the form of opportunities and synchronicities that allow us to make a complete change in our lives.

ESTABLISHED A DEADLINE FOR EACH GOALS

During the first two steps of the process, you should have come up with a list of goals and then narrowed them down. You should now have a shorter list of goals that you are excited about and that you are very attached to. Strong motivation and excitement are very important when it comes to achieving your goals, and they can help a lot to speed up the process of achieving these goals. You can also use the strong feelings you've had to get through challenges and setbacks as you work to reach your goals. Following this, you'll group your goals into short-term, medium-term and long-term ones. You'll also give each of your goals an end date.

DAILY GRATITUDE

Morning: I am grateful for:

I'm looking forward to:

Daily Affirmations:

Evening: Good things that happened today:

Things I can do to make tomorrow even better to reach my goal:

REGROUPING YOUR GOALS

Regrouping your goals into realistic time frames is essential for achieving them. A short-term goal is one that you believe you will be able to complete within the next three months. These goals may necessitate some effort to achieve, so stay realistic and work within your current realm of possibilities. As your confidence grows and you begin to see the benefits, you can start to stretch your life and set larger short-term goals. When you begin regrouping your goals, you should start with your long-term goals and work your way backward to the present. This will allow you to identify more medium-term and short-term goals that you will need to achieve to complete your long-term goals.

MEDIUM-TERM GOALS

Medium-term goals are those you expect to be accomplished in the next year. Put together a list of one to five objectives you hope to achieve in the upcoming year. These are significant objectives that may take some time to complete and may necessitate new skills. These aren't objectives that require a radical shift in your way of life.

SHORT-TERM GOALS

Write down your short-term goals, things you want to do in the next three months. It would help if you were realistic about your goals on this list of things to do. They must be able to be done, but not easy to do. You want to set goals that will push you a little and show you when you've done them. This way, you can see when you've done them. People who achieve their goals are more likely to achieve bigger, more long-term goals in the future when they have more confidence in their abilities.

LONG-TERM GOALS

Long-term goals are things you want to do in the next five to 10 years and more. Write down one to five long-term goals. If you have a lot of big goals, you should put them on this list. They may take a long time or require you to do other things first. Short and medium-term goals are easier to achieve when you meet them more quickly. You may find that some of your long-term goals can be put on your list of medium-term goals as well. This is because you have reached your goals quickly and have come to believe that you can get any goal you set for yourself.

“

You'll never know what you can do, unless you give it a try. Goals have the power to help you reach new heights and achieve your dreams.

”

chapter seven

PLAN FOR SUCCESS

The secret to success is having a plan.

If you want to be successful, you need to have a plan and stay on track. Make sure to set goals for yourself and work towards them, and you'll be on the right path! The secret to success is having a plan. By planning out your goals and keeping them in mind, you can keep yourself on the right path to making them a reality. Effective time spent up front on planning usually means less wasted time and effort spent on monitoring whether your goals are working and on remedying any shortcomings.

If you have goals in mind, you're already ahead of the game. But having goals isn't enough to ensure you'll reach them; if you're going to get where you want to be, you need a plan for success that you can actually stick with. Below are the guides for you to achieve your goals. Find what works for you and make it part of your regular routine. And if your efforts aren't producing results, keep looking until you find a system that helps give your goals the boost they need to really take flight.

CREATING AN ACTION PLAN

For each of your goals, you need to write down a plan of action. Your action plan will include all the steps you will need to take to reach your goals, so you know what to do next. In spite of the fact that you may not know all of the steps you will need to take, it's still a good idea to write down as many as you can. In the future, you can add more steps to your plan as they become more clear to you. To start making an action plan, you need to think about your goals and figure out how to reach them. For example, if you want to start a business, write down your research there are a lot of things you need to include in your action plan. Part of a plan to become a business owner is research.

- Take a business ethics course to improve your skills
- Read books in your genre to improve your craft
- Learn how successful hustlers achieved their success
- Spend two hours a day brainstorming, eliminating interruptions
- Find out how investors/hustlers become so successful

Each of the action steps you come up with are like a mini-goals. Some of these mini-goals may have to be done in a particular order, but others may be done with others. Planning for meaningful and worthwhile goals takes a lot of thought. To quickly reach your goals, pay attention to the small things. As soon as you start writing things down, your mind will begin to put things in order, allowing you to come up with new ideas that you hadn't thought of before.

BRAINSTORMING

Action brainstorming can help identify what things are helping or stopping you from achieving your goals.

MY GOAL

STOP DOING

DO LESS OF

KEEP DOING

DO MORE OF

START DOING

CREATE A DAILY SUCCESS PLANNER

Making a daily success planner will help you get into a routine and help you set aside time to work on your goals. Thanks to the daily success planner you make, you will get more done during the day. It can also help you quickly make your dreams come true. A daily success planner will help you set aside time each day to do the most important things to you so that you keep moving toward your goals. You can either make your success planner at the start of each day or the end of each day for the next day.

If you want to make a daily success planner, write down the names of three of your most important goals or projects. Do this on a piece of paper. These could be short-term, medium-term, or long-term goals or a mix of the three as we discussed in previous chapter. You should write down up to five steps for each project to help you reach your goal. If people help you with the projects, make sure you write down their names. Next, you need to write down the names of the people who want to hear from you. At the bottom of the page, write down your most important tasks for the day. Do these tasks, no matter what. If you want to reach your goals, you can use a simple tool like a daily success planner to help. It can help you make miracles happen in your life and help you achieve anything you want.

CONSISTENT DAILY ACTIONS

you need to take consistent daily actions toward your goals if you want to be successful in achieving them. Small, regular, daily actions will mount up to massive results over time because they will bridge the future you want. Many people start a great plan but quickly abandon it at the first hurdle they encounter. So, it is important to commit to yourself that you will not be someone who gives up at the first setback. To get the maximum results from a minimum effort, you have to take consistent daily actions toward your goals. Merely taking a single small step every day over a year can add up to a lot of progress toward achieving your biggest goals.

MY SUCCESS PLAN

DEADLINE: ACHIEVED: ☐

BREAK DOWN YOUR BIG GOAL INTO 3 MINI GOALS

MINI GOAL 1:	MINI GOAL 2:	MINI GOAL 3:

ACTION STEPS:	ACTION STEPS:	ACTION STEPS:
☐ ____________	☐ ____________	☐ ____________
☐ ____________	☐ ____________	☐ ____________
☐ ____________	☐ ____________	☐ ____________
☐ ____________	☐ ____________	☐ ____________
☐ ____________	☐ ____________	☐ ____________
☐ ____________	☐ ____________	☐ ____________

DAILY GOAL PLANNER

TOP PRIORITY

TODAY'S 3 MAJOR TASKS

TODAY'S 3 MINOR TASKS

PLAN OF ACTION

8:00 AM

9:00 AM

10:00 AM

11:00 AM

12:00 PM

1:00 PM

2:00 PM

3:00 PM

4:00 PM

5:00 PM

6:00 PM

NOTE TO SELF

How bad do you want it

HARNESSING THE POWER OF MIND MAPPING

Mind mapping is a great way to help you come up with ideas for your next steps. This is how to get your ideas and thoughts on paper. It can help you think creatively and logically to come up with new ideas. Map out your thoughts with mind mapping to get more important ideas about the plan you are making. It makes your brain think in new and creative ways, which helps you come up with ideas.

When you create a mind map, you make a very well-organized map that is very similar to how your brain works. It's a good idea to use mind mapping to write down your ideas in any order you come up with. Later, you can move them around to make them make more sense. Your goal should be your first thought. This is your main idea. It's from there that you can branch out from your goal. You can think about all the steps you'll need to take to reach your goal. The main branches that lead from your main idea are your key thoughts. The secondary branches show your secondary thoughts about your key thoughts.

Start making mind maps for each of your goals now that you know how important they are for your action plan. Each of your goals can be achieved by following the process. Keep in mind that as you work toward your goals, you should check the mind maps you made to see any new steps you need to take. Almost all of your mind maps will change as you start to think of new ideas.

PLANNING

RESEARCH

MIND
MAPPING
EXERCISE 1

TO DO LIST

EVALUATION

MIND MAPPING EXERCISE 2

PLANNING

RESEARCH

TO DO LIST

EVALUATION

BLOCK OUT TIME FOR YOUR GOALS

Start setting aside a certain amount of time each day where you only work on your goals. This will help you achieve more in your life. Without this, it will take you along to reach your goals. If you don't set aside this time, leaving everything up to chance, you won't be able to work on the steps you set out for yourself to reach your goals. To work on your goals, you need to set aside time for them. When you are working on your goals, you should try to keep things as simple as possible. You'll have to turn off your phone, stop using email, and close your social media accounts when you do this.

WINNING BACK TIME

You may think that you don't have enough time to work on your goals. This isn't true. The only way to get back your time is to make a few minor changes. For example, to get to bed earlier, you could turn off the TV an hour earlier than usual. This means you'll be able to get up earlier to work on your goals before going to work. High-performers know how to manage their time and don't have any problems getting rid of things that don't help them reach their goals. In the beginning, when you start to manage your time more efficiently, it may feel like you're giving up a lot of your freedom. However, you'll soon find out that it doesn't work that way. Remove the things that don't benefit you or your family, and you'll be left with what's most important. You will find that you have more time to make and live the life you want, rather than having your life be created for you. Your newfound free time will also surprise you. You can spend it on the important things to you and make your life happy.

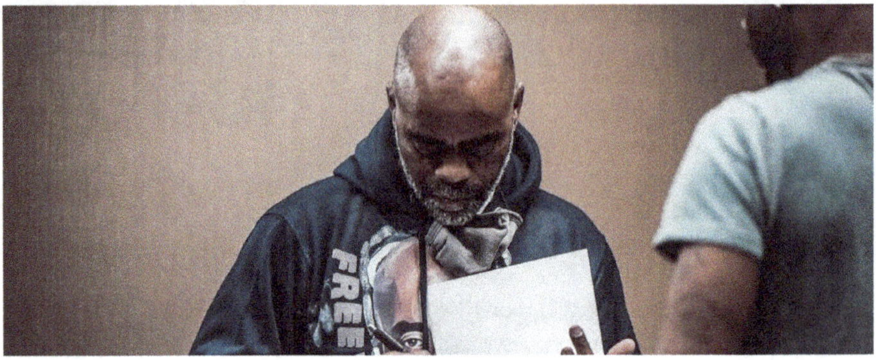

RECHARGE YOUR ENERGY AND FOCUS

It is very important how you feel about what you can do. When you have a clear mind, great things happen. However, if you're always tired, you won't get as much done during the day. After a long day, your body starts to run out of energy. This can make you feel tired and stressed out at the end of the day. This is how life works. It's still possible, though, to learn how to keep your energy up as you go about your day. It's better to take short breaks during the day than to try to do a lot of things at once. By taking short breaks during the day, you'll have more energy and be able to do more at the end of the day. Study: Each break should be between two and three minutes long and taken every hour. This lets you keep up a high level of performance in all of your jobs. It's better to take a short break every hour to let your mind recharge and refresh, so you can get back to work with more focus and energy when you start again.

CHANGE THE WORLD AROUND YOU BY TAKING ACTION

In the beginning, when you start taking steps toward your goals, you might begin to notice coincidences. It's also possible that your environment will respond to you differently than before. No matter what you want to achieve, you have to be ready for problems. They might make you think you're going in the wrong direction at first. As a result, you will always have to make some changes inside yourself to reach any big goal. When you go through things that make your life more complex, it shows you that you can get your goal. The bigger the goal you set, the more difficult it will be to reach it, The truth is, if you don't face challenges that make you grow, it's almost impossible to reach your goals. It's the challenges that make you grow and change to do anything in your life.

CREATING ROUTINES FOR GOAL SETTING

A routine is a plan of action that you follow each day to help you accomplish your goals. Having a routine can be helpful in goal setting because it helps you stay on track and makes sure that you are always working towards your goal. Having a routine also helps keep you accountable, which can be helpful in reaching your goals.

One way to create routines to help accomplish your goals is to find a time each day when you can dedicate yourself to working on your goal. Designating time for brainstorming or mind mapping is critical to staying focused. This may be in the morning, afternoon, or evening whichever one works best for you. Once you have found this time, you can create a routine for yourself that will help you stay on track. Some things you may want to include in your routine are:

- Checking in on your goal
- Planning what you will do that day to work towards your goal
- Doing whatever it is that you planned

Creating a routine like this can help keep you accountable and make sure you are always working towards your goal.

If you find it difficult to stick to your routine, here are some tips that may help:

- Make sure your routine is realistic and achievable. If it is too difficult or unrealistic, you are less likely to stick to it.
- Start with a small routine and gradually add more tasks as you become more comfortable with it. This will make it less daunting and easier to stick to.
- Motivate yourself by setting goals within your routine. This can help keep you driven and focused on what you want to achieve.
- Reward yourself for completing tasks within your routine. This will help keep you motivated and encouraged to keep going.

If your routine is not working, there are a few things you can do to try and fix it. Here are some tips:

- Make sure your routine is realistic and achievable. If it is too difficult or unrealistic, you are less likely to stick to it.
- Start with a small routine and gradually add more tasks as you become more comfortable with it. This will make it less daunting and easier to stick to.
- Motivate yourself by setting goals within your routine. This can help keep you driven and focused on what you want to achieve.
- Reward yourself for completing tasks within your routine. This will help keep you motivated and encouraged to keep going.

Routine

I am going to:	I am going to:
I am going to:	I am going to:
I am going to:	I am going to:

Routine

I am going to:

I am going to:

I am going to:

I am going to:

I am going to:

I am going to:

Routine

I am going to:	I am going to:
I am going to:	I am going to:
I am going to:	I am going to:

Focus On

I am going to focus on :

I am going to focus on:

I am going to focus on:

I am going to focus on:

I am going to focus on:

I am going to focus on:

Focus On

I am going to focus on :	I am going to focus on:
I am going to focus on:	I am going to focus on:
I am going to focus on:	I am going to focus on:

Focus On

I am going to focus on :

I am going to focus on:

I am going to focus on:

I am going to focus on:

I am going to focus on:

I am going to focus on:

chapter eight

DEVELOP A POSITIVE MINDSET

DEVELOP A POSITIVE MINDSET

Developing a positive mindset is an essential step towards achieving your goals. When we talk about having a positive mindset, we're talking about being optimistic and having faith in yourself and your abilities.

Having faith in yourself and your abilities means knowing that you will do what it takes to achieve your goals because when you have that positive mindset, there's no other way to feel. This belief in yourself is what gets you there in the end, so don't let anyone tell you differently!

You might be wondering how this is any different from a traditional mindset? Think of it this way; if you were trying to get into shape, a positive attitude would be all about being able to see the bright side of things. Surrounding yourself with people who will support you on your journey instead of constantly finding excuses for why not, staying hopeful about what might happen instead of thinking about how much worse things could get, and always moving forward rather than dwelling on past mistakes.

> If you set your mind to doing something and think positively about it then things will go well and you will achieve your goal. Some of the most successful people have been able to reach their goals by thinking positively no matter what happened around them

It can be easy to get discouraged when things do not go as planned but it is important to remember that these things happen and that not all things are in our control. If we let ourselves get caught up in negative thoughts we will eventually let these emotions overwhelm us causing us to give up on our dreams

Positive Mindset

Don't focus on what could go wrong.

01

When you set out to achieve a goal, the most productive thing you can do is focus on what needs to be done to reach it. It's easy to get so caught up in the steps that you lose sight of your end goal and make yourself anxious. You've got to have faith that things will work out as long as you do what's needed in order for them to work out. Think of it this way: You're not trying not to fail; you're trying to succeed.

Be willing to risk failure by taking action toward your goals.

02

You have to take action toward your goals. You can't just sit there and wish for something better for yourself; you have to go out there and work for it. You might not always get positive feedback or even positive results from your actions. In fact, sometimes you won't get anything at all—but if you're willing to risk failure, if you're willing to take an action that could potentially result in a negative outcome, then I think that's the first step toward success. After all, failure is a natural part of life, and sometimes it takes a lot of effort for even the smallest of things to go our way.

Find a role model who has already succeeded despite failing at times.

03

As you begin your journey to success, you may feel scared. You might worry that you can't accomplish your goals because you've failed in the past. You might fear that if you fail, it's all over. If this is how you're feeling, remember this: everyone who succeeds has failed at some point along the way. It doesn't matter whether it was just a few times, or if it was every time they tried something new. The key is to never give up. There are plenty of examples of people who have failed repeatedly but still managed to succeed spectacularly in the end. It's important to find a role model who has already succeeded despite failing at times. You'll be able to see that it's okay to fail as long as you don't quit.

Programming Your Subconscious Mind

04

Your subconscious mind has two parts, the conscious and the unconscious. The unconscious mind is the one that does all the work for you. It controls breathing, heart rate, digestion, and even long division. The conscious mind processes information from your senses and sends messages to the body's muscles so that you can move. To set goals, we must first get in touch with our subconscious minds.

An incredible power resides in your subconscious mind, but most people don't know how to access it. The subconscious mind is responsible for all of your automatic behaviors like breathing, blinking, and digestion. It also regulates emotions and controls your body's chemistry and hormones. Moreover, it stores all of your memories, which means that if you learn something new, the brain will automatically apply the lesson to any situation. Best of all, everything that happens in the world around you goes directly into your subconscious mind and can be accessed anytime.

Do not expect instant results, but the payoff of a more positive life can be worth the effort. You may want to try some of these techniques after doing these exercises ;

Committing to your goals

A successful approach to achieving any goal starts with a solid foundation and commitment. To start committing yourself to your goals, the following road map can be used as a guide:

Step 1: Identify Your Goals – Begin by reflecting on what you want to achieve and why. Get clear on what it is that you are aiming for and write it down. Having clearly articulated, written goals gives you something tangible to work towards and allows you to visualize success.

Step 2: Set A Timeline – Figure out when exactly you want to accomplish each goal by making an achievable timeline that is realistic and specific. This will help you break your larger ambitions into achievable steps which will assist in keeping yourself accountable.

05

Step 3: Break Down Your Goal – To make sure that you stay on track, create a step-by-step plan of exactly how you will reach each goal. The more detailed the plan, the better equipped you'll be to stay focused on the task at hand and make steady progress in reaching each milestone along the way.

Step 4: Monitor Your Progress – Set up a tracking system or find an accountability partner who can help monitor your progress and provide feedback throughout this journey. Regular check-ins can provide motivation as well as give recognition for milestones achieved during this process.

Step 5: Celebrate Successes & Learn from Mistakes – As with any journey, there will be successes along with setbacks. Celebrate these successes no matter how small they may appear, as this reinforces positive behavior that helps keep your motivation high throughout this process. When mistakes occur, use them as learning experiences rather than points of discouragement; remember that failure is part of growth and serves as fuel for further determination in achieving success.

Discipline

06

Discipline is an essential component of successfully achieving any meaningful goals. Without it, one may struggle to maintain focus and consistency in their efforts, which can lead to frustration and a lack of progress. By its very nature, discipline is the act of focusing your attention and energy on consistently working hard toward the desired outcome. It involves deliberately adhering to a specific set of behaviors or actions – often over extended periods of time – in order to push oneself toward the desired outcome.

One key advantage to having discipline when pursuing goals is that it helps build momentum and prevents procrastination. When you are disciplined enough to stay focused on the tasks at hand even when you don't feel like it, you will find that progress happens faster than if you were to give in to distractions or lazy behaviors. Additionally, when you practice discipline regularly, it becomes easier for you to stay on course and make steady progress since it becomes second nature for you to stick with your goals without needing constant external motivation or reminders.

Further, having discipline can also help create better self-control habits which will serve you well in other areas throughout life. With increased self-control, we become better able to resist temptations that otherwise could easily derail our plans and success. This can include anything from staying away from unhelpful activities such as smoking or drinking excessively, all the way up to better managing our finances or improving our diets by avoiding junk food or overeating.

Finally, another major benefit of discipline when trying to reach goals is that it gives us greater confidence as we measure our accomplishments over time and see tangible results from our efforts. This motivates us further while also reinforcing positive habits that naturally bring forth more successful outcomes each day! When we take pride in seeing the fruits of our efforts come alive through discipline, this creates a powerful sense of satisfaction which can propel us further into achieving great things with even more enthusiasm!

OVERCOME LIMITING BELIEFS

Limiting beliefs are beliefs that stop us from taking action on things we want in our lives because they are not true. In this exercise, you will learn how to identify which beliefs limit you and how to focus on what is possible rather than your limiting beliefs in order to develop a positive mindset.

A Belief that is holding you back:

e.g It's hard to reach that goal.

Where did this belief come from?

How is this belief harmful?

What is a better alternative for this belief? Empowering my new belief to reach my goal.

THOUGHT PATTERN

Your mindset determines everything in your life, like the way you react to things, and the way you believe that you are able to achieve your aims and goals. In this exercise, we will help you learn to generate good thoughts and create a new habit of good thinking. It looks like a simple exercise, and at first, it might seem difficult, but with determination and perseverance, you're going to break through to new levels and achieve your goals.

NEGATIVE → POSITIVE

NEGATIVE → POSITIVE

NEGATIVE → POSITIVE

NEGATIVE → POSITIVE

AFFIRMATIONS

Affirmations have many powerful benefits to help you achieve more in life and it helps help you learn to manage your emotions, improve self-image and develop a positive mindset. Start improving your life and develop positive mindset by writing down these I AM Affirmations.

I AM ...

I AM ...

I AM ...

I AM ...

GOAL MANIFESTATION

Having a strong feeling of success is an amazing feeling and allows us to take on any challenge. If we can develop a positive mindset about our abilities and the world around us, we will find ourselves much more successful in our endeavors. Start this manifestation exercise and embody the feeling of reaching your goals.

MANIFESTATION

VISUALIZATION:

I see

I have

I feel

MY DAILY AFFIRMATIONS

1. ______

2. ______

3. ______

CONSISTENT ACTION PLAN

1. ______

2. ______

3. ______

chapter nine

TAKE ACTION BUILD A SUPPORT TEAM

TAKE ACTION, BUILD A SUPPORT TEAM

Family

Building a support network of people around you is important when you are trying to invest in yourself because it gives you a sense of security and encouragement. First, having a family network of support can help to provide motivation and encouragement. When you are working towards something, it can often be difficult to push yourself out of your comfort zone. It can be hard to stay motivated and focused on your goals. Having the support of your family can give you the extra boost you need to keep going and make sure you are staying on track. Second, having family around you can provide you with the resources and guidance you need to reach your goals. It can be helpful to have someone you can turn to for advice or guidance when you are working on something. Having a family that you can rely on can help you to stay on track and reach your goals. Third, having a family network of support can provide emotional support. When you are working on something, it can be easy to get discouraged or overwhelmed. Having a family that is there to listen and provide emotional support can make all the difference. It can help to remind you why you are investing in yourself and help to keep you going when things get tough. Finally, having a family network of support can help you to feel connected and loved. When you are investing in yourself it can be easy to feel isolated and alone. Having family around you can help to make sure you never feel isolated and can provide you with the love and support you need to keep going. Having a family network of support is incredibly important when you are investing in yourself. It can provide you with the motivation, resources, guidance, and emotional support you need to stay on track and make sure you are reaching your goals. When you have family, friends, professionals, mentors, community, and colleagues to rely on and confide in, it can help you to stay focused, motivated, and inspired.

Friends

Having family in your support network can provide you with the emotional support, understanding, and unconditional love that you need to stay positive and energized. They can also provide practical help and advice when you need it. Having friends in your support network can be equally helpful, as they can be a source of positive reinforcement and caring companionship that can make you feel valued and appreciated. They can provide you with comfort, understanding, and a sense of security that can make all the difference in helping you stay the course. Having someone to talk to about the issues or struggles you are facing can help you gain clarity and perspective, enabling you to make decisions with greater assurance.

TAKE ACTION, BUILD A SUPPORT TEAM

Aside from emotional support, having friends around you can also be beneficial in terms of practical advice and assistance. When you are investing in yourself, you may need help with research, problem-solving, and decision-making. Having a knowledgeable and supportive group of friends who can offer their insight can be invaluable. Finally, having a support network can be beneficial in terms of financial assistance. When you are investing in yourself, you may need to make some large purchases or take risks that require a financial commitment. Having friends who are willing to lend you money or help you out financially can be an invaluable resource. In short, having a strong support network of friends and family around you when you are investing in yourself can make all the difference in terms of success. Not only can they provide you with emotional and practical support, but they can also be a source of financial assistance when needed.

Professionals

Professionals, such as therapists, coaches, and advisors, can provide you with specialized knowledge, resources, and tools to help you reach your goals. Building a support network of professional people around you when you are trying to invest in yourself is incredibly important for a number of reasons. Firstly, having a network of professionals provides you with a valuable resource that can be tapped into for advice, guidance, and support when needed. It is beneficial to have a network of people who have experience in the same field as you, who have been successful in their own endeavors, and who can provide you with the encouragement and direction you need. Additionally, having this network can help to give you a better understanding of the industry, The opportunities available to you, and the resources available to help you progress. Having a support network of professional people around you also gives you a sense of security. Knowing that those around you have your best interests at heart and are willing to support you can be incredibly reassuring when you are trying to make a success of yourself. It gives you a sense of belonging and a feeling that you are not alone on your journey. It also provides a source of motivation and inspiration and can help to reinforce the belief that you can achieve your goals. Finally, having a support network of professionals around you can help to give you a greater sense of confidence and self-belief. Knowing that you have the backing of experienced people who have achieved success in their own endeavors can be incredibly empowering. It can also help to boost your self-esteem, as you will feel more in control of your future and more capable of taking on new challenges.

TAKE ACTION, BUILD A SUPPORT TEAM

Mentors

Having a mentor in your support network can be invaluable, as they can provide you with guidance and wisdom based on your own experience and successes. They can also offer you a fresh perspective and help you to stay on track. Building a support network of mentors around you is an important part of investing in yourself. Having a team of knowledgeable and experienced professionals who can provide guidance and support can be invaluable to your success. Here are a few reasons why it's important to build a support network of mentors when you are trying to invest in yourself:

1. Access to Knowledge and Experience: When you have mentors around you, you have access to their knowledge and experience. This can help you make better decisions and avoid costly mistakes. Your mentors can provide valuable insights and guidance that will help you to reach your goals faster.

2. Improved Self-Awareness: Mentors can help you gain a better understanding of yourself and your strengths and weaknesses. They can provide you with feedback and help you to identify areas where you need to improve. This can help you to become more self-aware and to better assess your capabilities and limitations.

3. Positive Support: When you have mentors around you, you have access to positive support and encouragement. This can help to boost your confidence and motivation, which can be invaluable when you are tackling difficult tasks or trying to make difficult decisions.

4. Increased Networking Opportunities: Having mentors around you can open up new networking opportunities. They can introduce you to people in their networks and help you to make valuable connections.

5. Improved Problem-Solving: With the help of your mentors, you can develop better problem-solving skills. They can offer advice and help you to think outside the box when it comes to tackling complex problems. Building a support network of mentors can be a great way to invest in yourself. It can provide you with access to knowledge and experience, improved self-awareness, positive support, increased networking opportunities, and improved problem-solving skills. Having mentors around you can be an invaluable asset to your success.

TAKE ACTION, BUILD A SUPPORT TEAM

Community

.Getting involved with your community can also be beneficial, as it can provide you with the opportunity to meet new people, learn new skills, and make valuable connections. Finally, having colleagues in your support network can offer you mentorship, support, and advice in your area of expertise.

It provides you with a support system and resources to help you make wise decisions and stay motivated. It also gives you access to advise from people who have been there and done that, which can be invaluable in learning from their experiences. Having a community of like-minded individuals around you can help you set and achieve goals, and provide you with accountability to make sure you stay on track.

Your community can also serve as a source of motivation, as you can draw inspiration from the successes of others and learn from their mistakes. In addition, having a community around you can serve as a source of encouragement and reassurance. It can be difficult to remain confident when you're investing in yourself and sometimes, a few words of encouragement can go a long way in helping you stay focused and positive.

Finally, having a community also provides you with a platform to share your successes and celebrate your accomplishments. This can be incredibly rewarding and help to maintain your motivation levels over the long term. In conclusion, building a community around you when you are trying to invest in yourself is essential for staying motivated and achieving success. It provides you with a support system, advice, accountability, motivation, encouragement, and a platform to share your successes.

Colleagues

Overall, having a strong support network of family, friends, professionals, mentors, community, and colleagues can make a huge difference when you are trying to invest in yourself. Not only can it make you feel more secure, but it can also help you to stay motivated and inspired on your journey.

Support Network

Family :	Friends:
Professionals:	Coach/Mentors:
Community:	Colleagues:

THANK YOU

Setting goals is one of the best things you can do for yourself. By following the steps in this book, you've decided to take full responsibility for your own life and start living the life you truly want. You can start now. If you follow the steps and advice, you can set smart goals, break free from negative thoughts about yourself, reprogram your mindset, and become a high performer in reaching your dreams. Use your goals as a source of inspiration and to help you get where you want to go in life. It is important to keep going and not let these short-term setbacks stop you from achieving your life's most important goals. Everyone can achieve their goals. It only takes a lot of small steps and a lot of motivation to achieve your goals.

.I hope you get something out of reading this workbook. Continue your journey to remaining accountable for achieving your goals by tracking your progression through my online app called the Vision Tracker. Sign up for the year today.

Freewayricky &

Mychosia Nightingale

VT
VISION TRACKER

NIGHTINGALE
LEADERSHIP ACADEMY
BUILDING LEADERS

Courses, Books & Merchandise can be purchased at
freewaymillionairesclub.com
freewayrickyross.com
mychosia.com

Personal Development & Goal Setting
Life Coaching Services available

www.ingramcontent.com/pod-product-compliance
Lightning Source LLC
LaVergne TN
LVHW050818061126
851857LV00012B/861
9798888955789